Gently Back
My Beloveds

By
Julia Abdey Wade

GENTLY BACK MY BELOVEDS

Table of Contents

Dedication

I tend to go along with life day by day, taking each moment as it comes. I know the experiences I've had are real. They are not figments of my imagination. They are not wishful thinking.

They *happened.*

There are many signs—too many—that prove to me I am not alone in my thoughts and desires.

It would be beautiful if *man* could come together, just once. Acting as a body of thought. Talking honestly about the things that might be important to the well-being of the *hereafter.*

Are we meant to play a greater role in the universe?

I believe we are.

Here we are, my gentle people—
I have set myself a task,
Your love and understanding
Are all the things I ask.
Search your hearts, look high, look low,
Forget the material hates you know.
Think soft, think gentle, find peace,
Let all the turmoil of the mind cease.
Find love, pure white dove.
Calm, serene, hush my child, hush,
Do not cry, let us sing a lullaby.
Peace, peace, look to the light,
No more fight, no more fight—
Just peace.

In loving memory of all my beloveds
who have gone to their spiritual rest.
And heartfelt thanks to RON,
who shares my love of Angels and offers his spiritual guidance.

About The Author

Whilst I have loved writing over the years, I have never tried publishing before, apart from bringing up my family and working to make ends meet. I have thoroughly enjoyed researching my father's family name of Abdey. I have made many friends and between us we have built several trees, one going back to 1345. It is great to think that we can unite spirit on a material level, we can appreciate each other and know that we are all human with trials and tribulations.

Introduction

It is my belief that the universe is made up of many, many levels of understanding. We talk about heaven and earth as though that's all there is—just the two levels—but what if there are more? As soul progresses through the earthly plane and then pause in heaven, many return to take part again in the classrooms of Earth. But what about those who remain in the heavenly state? Can they go on to another dimension of thought?

Let me introduce myself. I am *ENERGY—NRG* for short. I occupy areas in the universe unknown even to thought itself. Thought eventually becomes spirit. And spirit? It takes on vehicles—bodies— that present themselves on a planet named Earth.

Part of *thought* believes Earth became Earth by breaking away from the safety of universal space. But until these vehicles—human minds—open just a little more to greater understanding, the planet will not lift. There is so much to know. Even I, *NRG*, have far to go.

I will descend a few rungs on that ladder at a later time. For now, I remain hidden—waiting until a great mind realizes the potential in introducing their theories to whatever powers may listen and help carry things further.

So hush now, Thought. Rest for a while. I do not know how long, because *I* do not know. I'm not even sure of myself. I will simply take advantage of the silence and rest—sending out gentle parts of myself in the hope that one day I will be found.

In the meantime, enjoy the level of the human mind—but be kind to yourselves. For I wait in humility, hidden, watching peacefully. One day, you will know me.

There is a possibility that, far in the future, when my cover is revealed, words will no longer be in command. Instead, we will speak in symbols, in letters, or through a simple *knowing* within one's own mind. Life will move as one, just gently controlling the order of the universe—until the next step reveals itself.

While I am *ENERGY*, it is *NRG* who will find me. Let me whisper for life to hear. Let me call out and see who listens:

Hush, gently back, my beloveds. Gently back...

No response? Then I must shout—

*****

Chapter 1

Our little Atom—who we named "God" in my book *Heaven to Earth*—eventually realized that his first creations were returning to "him" far too quickly. "He" had to devise a plan. The earth wasn't moving; it wasn't lifting to its rightful place in the universe. He summoned all his Angels—atoms who had awakened—to assist "him" in his plight. His little piece of "Heaven" soon lit up with beautiful strings of gold, their goal to touch the planet Earth and allow spirit/soul to descend and be reborn. Many wanted to try again. Rebirth became known as reincarnation.

One such soul who left the security of heaven was a gentleman named John Edward Masefield. He was an English poet and writer, born—according to Wikipedia—in 1878, in Ledbury, Hertfordshire. In adulthood, he spent many years at sea and eventually wrote numerous poems involving the ocean.

Interestingly enough, he possibly died in Cholsey, where he had married Constance de la Crommellin (1867–1960). They lived at Lollingdon Downs in Cholsey until 1917—a place where many of my ancestors are buried. Masefield became Poet Laureate in 1930 and held the title until his death. He was cremated, and his ashes were placed in Poets' Corner at Westminster Abbey.

Mr. Masefield wrote many poems, sonnets, and stories. He was certainly a very interesting person. In the 1920s, his family settled at Boars Hill, a rural setting near Oxford.

One verse I find particularly moving—one that I believe was found after his death—is this:

"Let no religious rite be done or read in any place for me, when I am dead. Burn my body into ash, scatter the ash, in secret into running water or on the windy down, Let none see and then thank God that there's an end of me."

Now, he was obviously a very deep thinker. Was this written in despair? Was he unhappy? Or was he suggesting that we are spirit/soul, held down by these vehicles we call bodies? I prefer the latter. It's part of my own realization. He was most likely in tune with the Infinite.

Another piece I find compelling—beside his love of the sea—is his reflection on reincarnation. He wrote:

"I hold that when a person dies, his soul returns again to earth, arrayed in some new flesh disguise, another mother gives him birth. With sturdier limbs and brighter brain the old soul takes the road again. Such was my belief and trust, this hand—this hand that holds the pen—has many a hundred times been dust, and turned as dust to dust again. These eyes of mine have blinked and shone in Thebes, in Troy, in Babylon. I know in my lives to be, my sorry heart will ache and burn and worship unavailingly the woman who I used to spurn and shake to see another have the love I spurned, the love she gave. And I shall know in angry words, in gibes and knocks and many a tear, a carrion flock of homing-birds, the gibes and scorns I uttered here. The brave word that I failed to speak will brand me dastard on the cheek. And as I wander on the roads, I shall be helped and healed and blessed. Kind words shall cheer and be as goads to urge the heights before unguised. My road shall be the road I made, all that I gave shall be repaid. So shall I fight, so shall I tread in this long war beneath the stars. So shall a glory wreath my head, so shall I faint and show the scars until this case, this clogging mold, be smithied all to kingly gold."

To me, it is a beautiful poem. It speaks volumes on the question of reincarnation and karma.

After reading it, I responded—at that time, just for my own records:

Dear John Masefield, *Bless this hand, show me the way to write a poem as grand— one that speaks a spiritual truth, one that is gentle, not uncouth. Come show me the way I may progress, to help each soul*

GENTLY BACK MY BELOVEDS

to their success. Let us speak in words of joy, to benefit all, "girl" or "boy." Let them partake of God's glory, let them know the true, true story.

Come, my friend, take my hand, lead us all to the Promised Land. Come in love and gratitude, for all the words spoken in platitude. Come, do not weep, do not cry, show us all that lullaby— for peace must dwell upon this Earth.

I have written many bits and pieces since 1967. My belief in reincarnation is very real. This, along with karma, makes perfect sense to me.

What a task our little Atom took on. He allowed many souls to become famous and worthy of recognition. He allowed many to try again. Others, he allowed to remain.

*****

Chapter 2

I would like to explain why I am so interested in this gentleman. I find I can identify with his thoughts. To explain, I have to bring in *astral traveling* and *out-of-body experiences* (OBEs).

It is said that we are made up of astral bodies—subtle forms that separate when the soul leaves the physical body to return to the Creator, whom we call "God." We refer to this separation as "death," though in truth, death simply means *change*.

Over many years, I've discovered that separation can happen without physical death. It can be done at will—with good practice. It can also occur when the body and mind are low or vulnerable.

For instance, one of my family members—very dogmatic in her beliefs—was quite set in her ways. She had her own methods of controlling life and, perhaps, the people around her through stern opinions. She was in the hospital after a hip operation and told me she became terrified when she suddenly found herself floating on the ceiling of the ward, looking down on her own body. I offer this as an example—someone very narrow-minded, yet it still happened to her.

"Unto thine own self be true."

I would love to share some of my own experiences. I know that if I lie, I am only lying to myself. For me, life is a great unfolding—an ongoing discovery of our possible evolution. I feel that even when man reaches his first goal of understanding, there are still many more challenges ahead. We are, in my estimation, *spirit*—spirit struggling to find purpose in all things.

It is the body and mind that suffer. The spirit—*the soul*—goes on. If we learn to control our thoughts, we can help our spirit travel peacefully, fulfilling the hopes of the Whole.

Please know, I never claim to be right. I don't know all the answers. I just love thinking for the joy of it. Everyone is entitled to their own

4

thoughts. We must follow our own intuition, accept what we can, and always keep an open mind. Unto your own self be kind—life is full of different ideas.

Planet Earth is a great schoolroom. And I do believe we need to have a foot in both dimensions: the physical plane and the hereafter. Could that be the answer to "heaven on earth"? Do we need to acknowledge both? For me, I'd say yes.

My first out-of-body experience happened when I was about five years old. I was at the dentist, and from above, I saw myself sitting in the chair being treated. I didn't understand what it was at the time.

Most of my other experiences came later—mainly in my forties. The first memorable one happened after I'd fallen asleep. I suddenly found myself standing by a wall in my bedroom. Then a window appeared—out of nowhere. Outside was a beautiful scene: a street filled with vintage cars, and a man playing music on his organ. I woke up in my bed. It was *not* a dream. I began referring to this kind of traveling as "visual dreams," but they were real. They happened. It was as though I had been there physically, in my material body.

In my teenage years, a Welsh aunt of mine bought a monkey from an organ grinder. Due to the distance between us, we rarely spent much time with her. Eventually, she brought the monkey to Torquay in Devon, staying with her youngest sister. My parents, my brother, and I would often visit them there.

When we all gathered, the monkey—Charlie—was a little horror! By the time we arrived, the curtains were already in tatters. (To be fair, my aunt probably put things right again afterward.)

Not far from the house was a wooded area. The blessed little soul escaped and ended up there! After many scratches and a bit of a struggle, Charlie was captured. (Psst... personally, I preferred the tortoise—even though it had the nerve to "spend a penny" on my nice green dress! LOL!)

My aunt's reason for bringing the monkey to her sister's home was because she intended to donate him to Paignton Zoo in Devon. For the life of me, I can't recall how she traveled with him. We didn't have cars in those days, so she must have gone by train. We used to visit Charlie at the zoo. Eventually, I think she gave up and settled for a dog—though, mind you, he was a fiery little soul as well!

Back to my OBEs—once I became aware of them, I was determined to try to initiate them at will. I'd had a few odd ones here and there, but one in particular stands out. I felt myself literally rise through the ceiling of my bedroom. Then I became conscious of sitting on a neighbor's rooftop, at the end of our avenue. I sat there quietly, just watching the sunrise.

My determination was quite strong—I followed the instructions before going to sleep. Eventually, I became aware that I was lying on my bedroom floor, completely unable to move. I knew what was happening. I asked to be taken further, but only managed to make it back to the top cover of my bed.

There was a time I shot out of my body entirely. I could observe the *astral cord*—the connection between our physical and subtle bodies. If I remember correctly, it was green—or maybe a brownish green. (Not so sure on that one now.)

In another experience, I found myself within a dragon. It felt like a ceremony, possibly during the Year of the Dragon. I heard the most beautiful voice singing. Within that visual dream, someone whispered, "That is the voice of Sappo Lene." When I came back to full consciousness, I looked up the name. Imagine my surprise when I found Sappho of Mytilene, from the Island of Lesbos. According to Wikipedia, she was an archaic Greek poet from either Eresos or Mytilene. Sappho wrote lyric poetry meant to be sung—she was often referred to as *The Tenth Muse* and *The Poetess*.

Legend says her parents were Skamandronymous and Cleis. She had siblings: Charaxus, Eurygius, and Lanichus. Though she's long been labeled a lesbian due to her connection to Lesbos, I would challenge that assumption. One tale claims she threw herself from the high cliffs into the sea after her love for the youth Phaon was not returned. In her mind, he preferred her slave, Melitta. She hasn't always been regarded as a lesbian—*time alters all things*.

So why have I included this beautiful soul from 615 BC? I ask myself—was my experience somehow tied to that time? Reading through her story and surviving poetry, I'd say she has traveled down the golden lifeline from our little Atom many times. She's most likely a very old soul. Was I there too? Intriguing.

Though I've read many books, I was never drawn to the arts or poetry. My reading has mostly been focused on spiritual awareness in the modern age—*the alternative to religion itself*. To me, religion is life. In earlier days, I might've been ducked in a medieval pond for saying so (big smiles).

Life is energy—some good, some bad—depending on which path we choose.

I fully believe that the Nazarene, along with his mother, belonged to an organization that studied the energies around us. He learned the true art of having one foot here and another in the hereafter. He, along with many teachers from alternative cultures, was—and still is—a great soul. He tried to show *man* the way. Many find deep upliftment from the knowledge that he still exists within the spiritual mind. *"Seek, and ye shall find."*

Back to my experiences—are you still with me?

Many will understand and accept what I'm sharing. But as I've said many times, *an experience is only an experience to the one experiencing it.* (Say that quickly now! *smiles*) To others, it may seem like nonsense. But OK—back to my lifeline from our little Atom. I'd bet I've had to learn many a lesson.

When I began my deeper research, I was already well into meditation. One morning, I sat comfortably in my chair and began my usual routine. Suddenly, I became aware that I was looking out *through* my skin. Everything was pink. I couldn't move my body. I looked at the armrest of the chair—and saw a very plump hand. I just sat there, knowing my husband would soon return for coffee. I asked to be brought back to normal. I was also aware of my black-and-white cat sitting on the back of the chair. But when I fully returned to consciousness, the cat wasn't there.

That opened up an interesting question:

Do animals have souls?

Can they also leave their bodies at will?

My answer: yes—to both.

Now, about that plump hand—I'll tell you another story that may be connected.

I'd been trying to convince my husband to let us get a dog. He kept saying, "No." (LOL) But I got my way when he wanted to change the car. My reply? "OK—but only if I can have a dog!" Guess who won? (Well... I suppose we both did!)

My daughter Sarah and I traveled out of town to buy a particular breed. The kennel we visited was in a terrible state. The poor little souls were sickly, and the place was full of disease. We walked out. On the way home, we saw an advert for dachshunds—beautiful little creatures. Loyal, if treated right.

And so, Sam came into our lives. At first, he was incredibly nervous. He wouldn't even eat. But he slowly gained trust and eventually took on a "wife" named Tania Rose. These two followed me everywhere. They'd sit near me as I meditated.

One day, I had a beautiful experience with them. I found myself *tripping*. I was lying on a bed. The dogs were there—one had puppies.

I knew I was actually *in* that situation. The floor was rough beneath me. I walked to the window to look outside, though I can't remember what I saw.

I moved out of the room—(Did I go down some stairs?)—and into a small kitchen. There was a mirror on the wall. Naturally, I went to look. I expected to see myself—how I normally looked. But to my complete wonder, I saw an *enormous, jolly-looking woman* wearing a white cap and apron.

Her reflection was me.

Was the plump hand I saw earlier *hers*? The image was as clear as anything I've ever seen.

Then, another face appeared—this time, a small cavalier-type figure. He had a moustache and wore a black hat. Oh boy—were they both past versions of me?

I was definitely in another dimension—no tension, just wonderment.

I left the mirror and stepped out the front door. There was no one around to have a "jaw." The house opposite seemed very close. I think I ventured in but came out quite soon. I walked along a narrow cobbled road. I didn't have a bag or any kind of load. I felt happy—I knew I wasn't dappy!

As I looked to the heavens, I saw a star shining brightly. (Did it shine twice nightly?) I could feel the star coming toward me. But back on the material plane, my blessed phone was ringing. I tried desperately to stay in the other dimension. I didn't want to leave my dogs behind in the past. My material mind just couldn't separate from them. Yet the phone kept ringing. The star was getting closer. Then— it all disappeared. I had to answer the phone.

Lesson learned: unplug the phone! (*Big smiles!*)

Now, there's a theory that if we travel far enough into the universe, we can witness the past, present, and future—simultaneously. In that moment, I was in the past, which became the present, and was then returned to the future. All at once, I realized: *everything still exists.*

There was a time I traveled back to the era of powdered wigs and such. I walked into a large room, and seated in one of the chairs was a woman in a beautiful dress of the time, wig and all. I passed by without speaking. In the hallway, a group of gentlemen were talking. No one addressed me until I tried to ascend the staircase. Then, a voice said, *"He isn't there."* Goodness knows who "he" was.

From that experience, I came back with the odd feeling that I was the ghost at that gathering. Or perhaps—I was just me.

As we are capable of traveling, it stands to reason that sometimes, when we see a figure, it may be a loved one simply looking in—just checking if everything's all right.

I know I've traveled to my daughter before, when she was in Exeter on holiday. We even chatted in the bathroom—in our astral bodies.

In another experience, I found myself aboard a ship. Looking in a full-length mirror—as I often do to see "who I am"—I saw an elderly woman in a long blue dress. My hair was gray. I walked down the stairs but sensed I wasn't very popular. At the bottom, I saw a long dining table, set for passengers. No one else was in sight.

Was I on the Titanic?

These experiences are so vivid. With each one, I was *actually there*, fully immersed, marveling at the event. I tried to make sense of the reality—dissecting my thoughts and feelings afterward.

But the beauty is when one receives proof.

Before I go on, let me share one experience that stayed with me for many years. On April 29, 1993, I wrote:

"In the early hours of the morning, when sleep becomes an astral trip, I spoke with my loved ones—those who had departed from this earth. I wandered away from their loving chatter and became aware of another matter. I found myself seated beside an elderly gentleman. He had a certain quiet beauty—well built, with gray hair and a full gray beard.

I felt it was my duty to sit with him and try to understand his purpose. I gently tried to read his soul. At that moment, he was alone—apart from the Whole. He allowed my inadequate tampering of his peace. I felt that he was there *for me*. Then he said, as clearly as could be:

'Don't forget what happened in 1945.'

And then—he was gone. I was awake again. But what happened in 1945?"

I've spent years trying to find a meaningful answer. You see, my philosophy is this: if I'm seeking—and I receive an answer—then I must try to *prove* the facts, just as I did with Sappho of Mytilene.

When I write, I tend not to research first. I allow the experience to emerge, and *then* I wait and see what truth it reveals. So—what happened in 1945?

I was born in 1940. That would've made me five years old. That same year, I had my first OBE—while at the dentist. I also had my tonsils removed. (Exciting, eh?)

Of course, 1945 marked the end of World War II. My father returned home soon after—but no, it wasn't that. I once had an OBE in which I followed a half–open-top car, vintage to the era. I was on a bicycle. We were traveling down Fore Street Hill in Exeter, Devon. Inside the car sat the Prime Minister—along with other political figures.

I didn't know the exact year, but with the war ending in 1945, *could it have been then?* I've tried researching it. I've even watched historical broadcasts on television—hoping to find a visual match. So far, I haven't been successful. But I keep asking the powers that be to please help me remember.

I now wonder if I've been given my answer.

Since deciding to share these experiences, I've watched a few of Mel Gibson's religious films. And to be honest—while I say I'm not religious—my writing suggests otherwise! Maybe I am. I consider myself a Free Thinker. To me, *religion is life itself.*

Life is meant to *be*, and how we handle our own destiny determines how far we journey into the unknown. Have I said that I believe totally in the Infinite? I do.

I feel it may be our duty to help uplift the planet—to return Earth to its rightful place in the universe, as I described in my book *Heaven to Earth.*

To me, this world is a schoolroom. Each soul takes different classes, depending on the lessons it feels it must learn. Did we choose those lessons before birth?

Who knows?

I believe that we each find our own pathway to fulfill the promises we made to ourselves *before birth*. It's the way we handle the trials and tribulations of life that becomes the true measure of our soul's maturity. We all need to believe in something—so we gravitate toward whatever uplifts us the most.

Still, we must always keep an open mind. We're constantly growing spiritually, in one direction or another. Most of us start at the beginning, climbing each golden rung to return to our origin. But even then, there will always be more rungs to climb—because the universe is infinite.

I wonder... how many golden ladders are there?

Mel Gibson has released a video suggesting that the Nazarene was not, in fact, a man. Many may find this hard to accept, as the idea was instilled in us from an early age—especially in school. That's certainly how I first came to know and love the story. I'm not sure how it's presented in schools today.

Still, I—along with many others—understand what he's trying to convey. We must learn to listen to our hearts, pay attention to our inner feelings, and follow the wisdom of the solar plexus. Ask for guidance. But always, always keep an open mind.

That single thought could be just one step on the rung of the spiritual ladder—the ladder that eventually leads us further into the unknown.

Mel G. has clearly done a great deal of research. He's guiding—but also acknowledging that the rungs are different for every soul.

***

So, back to 1945. What's the most recent insight I've discovered?

I have no doubt that some readers will already know what I'm about to say—and I'm going to stick with it.

In 1945, the Gnostic Gospels were discovered!

Thank you, Mel.

I've now ordered a book on these Gospels, as I believe they deal with reincarnation and karma. We know that many great teachers—from *all* cultures—were born to help souls navigate their ordeals here on Earth.

I was brought up in the Christian faith. But no, I was never made to go to Sunday school or attend church. My parents lived in the moment—doing their best to make ends meet. They gave my brother and me love and understanding. They were never demanding when it came to scripture or belief.

Still, the *whys and wherefores* of life always fascinated me.

***

As I've said, it's wonderful when one's OBEs are confirmed with proof.

Just imagine it—flying.

Soaring above and beyond, over the duck pond and into the great unknown.

In one such experience, I found myself in exactly that situation. There was a helper on either side of me—silent, but gently guiding. As I often do, I tried to look down to see what I was wearing. This time, I managed it. I looked at my feet and saw shoes with pointed toes—definitely from another era. Were they hand-stitched? I'm not sure.

Later, during a visit to an old English castle of repute, I came across a glass display cabinet—and inside it were the very same shoes. *Hey—did I borrow them and then return them? (grins)*

***

In another OBE, I found myself in a long room, with a great, old-fashioned conference table at the center. It was surrounded by an outer balcony. As I stood on that balcony, looking down into the courtyard, I saw one of my daughters walking—surrounded by many others, as though they were part of a gathering or procession of the time.

Fascinating.

***

I know many people have these kinds of experiences. Sometimes, they arrive as dreams—but not all dreams are the same. If you can recognize it, you'll *know* the difference between a dream and an experience.

Some experiences can seem frightening at first. But once you understand what's happening, you can truly begin to enjoy them.

***

There was a time when two helpers—one on each side—placed a cloak around my shoulders. They took me to another level of awareness. It was grim.

As I looked around, I noticed a skinless soul, just hanging onto a post, moaning. "He" seemed to be in great distress. Yet I felt protected—safe within the cloak they'd wrapped around me. I simply let them lead me through the scene.

Eventually, we arrived at a house. Inside was an aunt of mine who had passed on. In life, she wasn't particularly loved in her later years. But it's said that when we pass over, we often enter the situation we feel most *comfortable* in.

Was this aunt still unhappy—perhaps punishing herself by placing herself among suffering souls?

With awareness and realization, I believe she would eventually lift herself to a higher realm of understanding.

Sometimes, we really are our own worst enemies.

Just a small but interesting adventure—I once went through a fireplace.

Behind it was a small room filled with old treasures.

There was a Penny Farthing bicycle, which I imagine was a replica of the original.

It looked fragile, but clean and perfect. There was also a baby carriage, and other items I can't quite recall now. They were all neatly arranged along the walls.

It was fascinating—so many memories of a past once lived.

15

***

I've found myself traveling down country lanes—peaceful, winding, and green.

One place felt like an island. I was just sitting, taking in the view.

In the distance, another island waited.

All I can say is—I didn't need a passport or a ticket. It was free! (*Smiles*)

***

The feeling of being unable to move is often the beginning—or end—of a trip.

Once, I was lying on my side, unable to move, and there seemed to be movement behind me.

In my mind, I could hear voices.

Helpers were trying to take wings off my back.

***

Was I being punished? Or was I at the dentist?

I remember sitting in a chair, a contraption fitted on my head. Was it some form of torture?

Mind you—dentist and torture do go hand in hand (*lol!*).

***

In one of my OBEs, I floated into my two girls' bedroom.

They were arguing in spirit—not in body.

Later, I drifted to the top of my stairs and looked down.

You see, *most people do travel*—they're just not aware of it.

***

The house I lived in was split-level. The back entrance opened into a narrow lane.

One night, I found myself walking spiritually up that lane.

I came to the bottom level of the house and looked up toward the dining room window.

There, I saw a circle of spirit friends, standing and singing.

The sound was glorious—truly out of this world. The vision didn't last long, but the melody stayed within me.

There's a lovely chord to spiritual singing.

***

I've been taken out through the wall by spirit helpers before.

There's so much more to life than we realize, to be honest.

We miss so much—out of fear.

Fear of the unknown. Fear of religious teachings.

And it's all understandable.

Some astral dreams are prophetic.

The best way to know is to pay attention—to test them through time. Trial and error, so to speak.

***

Once, I was told that Death was going to call.

Since I was researching, it didn't alarm me.

A few days later, the phone rang.

The woman's name?

Mrs. Death.

***

On another occasion, I was standing at the end of a road by a garage. A helper stood beside me.

We watched as a car caught fire.

I asked if it was a particular person's car, but the helper told me, "Just watch."

Later, I found out that my young friend and her boyfriend were out on a trip—and their car did catch fire.

It wasn't as dramatic as what I'd seen—but still—it had been shown to me.

***

And once, I was standing at the end of a long room. On the right-hand side, there was an open door with a light shining through.

I noticed my uncle from Australia—he was blind. He seemed to be fumbling, as if searching for a way out.

Gently, I said, *"Go to the light."*

The following week, we found out that my dear uncle had passed.

I could say, in a way, that I had already said goodbye. And more beautifully—he had found the light.

From the depth of darkness,

There shone a light,

A tiny spark but oh so bright.

The darkness changed itself to day,

The light was sent to show the way.

Gently back my beloved, gently back.

*****

Chapter 3

It's said that reincarnation was once part of the Bible—before it was removed. According to some sources, including Wikipedia, it was Emperor Justinian the Great and his wife Theodora—ruling from 527 to 565—who feared the idea of rebirth. They wanted one life, one path, one chance. It was, as it often is, a power struggle. And just like today, fear played a central role.

But I often ask myself: if this life is truly the end, then why are we capable of traveling beyond it?

Why do so many of us receive insights into the spiritual world, even if only in fleeting moments or unexpected dreams? *Seek and ye shall find*, my friends. We're never alone—not really. We just keep ourselves tied to this earthly plane. Go within. It's not a sin. It might just be the very thing that saves you.

And what of love?

Love, in my opinion, is the force that overcomes all. It pushes us forward—toward healing, toward truth, and eventually, toward our soul's designated goal. But not all love is the same, is it?

There's the love of a child, a partner, a friend... and then there's sexual love, which seems to cause the most chaos of all. Jealousy, suspicion, control—why must love be policed? Shouldn't we all be allowed to have a friend of our choosing without being labeled or judged?

Here's something I wrote once:
A mother's love is a special kind,
One that comes from heart to mind.
A child's love is never failing,
On a cloud forever sailing.
A father's love engulfs them all,
Always there lest they fall.
And then... there's another kind entirely:

19

***

There once was a soul with plenty of money,
All was good and sweet as honey,
But in all his endeavor,
Although very clever,
A lot was he missing.
No loving, no kissing.
No comfort, no joy,
From a girl or a boy.
No marriage, no wife,
No love in his life.
Only his money,
That was as sweet as honey.

***

There are so many kinds of love. And if Earth truly is a schoolroom—as I believe it is—then each type of love comes with its own lesson. Some bring joy. Others bring fire. But all of them are purposeful. And maybe, just maybe, those experiences help us keep one foot in this world and the other in the Infinite.

Now, let's talk about dreams. Or rather, what I call *visual dreams*—those experiences that feel real, that *are* real in some deeper way. If we take reincarnation into consideration, perhaps we can begin to see the reason behind so many of our experiences. But reincarnation doesn't work alone. It walks hand in hand with karma.

Karma can be instant. A sudden consequence. Or it can be slow—something we've dragged from another lifetime into this one. Sometimes, I even wonder if we choose to carry someone else's karma as part of our soul contract. Before birth, did I say, *"Yes, I'll take this on for you"*?

Oh boy, what famous person might I have been?

Julius Caesar or just the court teaser? Romeo? Juliet? A pauper? A poet? A rogue or a priest? No matter the past lives, one truth remains:

we are responsible for the choices we've made—then and now. Karma weaves the threads across all of time.

The realms of light are within us all,

Be we short or be we tall.

I've often wondered—and I know I'm not alone—if the dream state is actually another dimension of reality. A quieter one. A parallel plane. Of course, not all dreams are cosmic in nature. Some are just echoes from our day: the small worries, the loud emotions, the leftover clutter of our minds.

But others? Others are sacred.

And they come bearing messages, lessons, or memories we've yet to fully understand.

No matter what the skeptics say—or how the world tries to explain things away—I cannot, and will not, deny my experiences.

My *Visual Dreams* are not fantasies or idle imagination. They are facts. Lived. Felt. Remembered. Some may scoff, others may smile politely, but to me, they are the soul's whispered truth.

Over the years, I've written countless pieces—many just for my own entertainment. But this one, in particular, has stayed with me. It poured out of me without effort, almost automatically. And still, it rings true, line by line:

***

I HAVE FOUND
The depth of the mind is mystery,
Is it myth, is it hope, or is it mastery?
The quality of life is heavenly,
Is it true, is it through, or continuously?
The peace of knowing
That spirit keeps growing,
The love at the thought
That spirit is taught.

21

Oh listen, my friends,
Our life never ends.
Have faith, be kind—It is all in the mind.

The miseries and sorrow,
Today and tomorrow,
Stop, just ponder,
Let your mind calmly wander.
Find peace and tranquility,
Not war and hostility.
We learn, you know,
Our minds will grow.
There was a beginning long ago,
How it started, I do not know.
Life evolved around and around,
Through thousands of years,
The theory is sound.
Each life we lived as best we could,
Departing each time from out of the wood.
Our deeds were accounted, then back we came—A different body, a
different name.
Each life we are meant,
As we are heavenly sent,
To fulfill a need,
To better a deed.
Then in final surrender,
In heavenly splendor,
Our spirit will stay,
Having found the way.
***

Over the years, I've written many pieces—just for my own entertainment.

The one above was one such piece. And yet, even now, I find I still hold those words dear.

22

Many of my writings came automatically, most of them without much thought at the time.

Now, as I reflect more deeply, I can honestly say that my experiences *do* mean something to me.

Are they just for my own gratification?

Who knows, eh?

I've spent money here, there, and everywhere—some of it wasted, some of it very worthwhile.

One such venture was a session with a psychic who offered past life readings.

All I did was send my name and address—and request a reading. The tape she sent back was very intriguing.

A friend of mine once commented that psychics always say what people *want* to hear.

And yes, some definitely do.

But this particular tape was given with no picture, no phone call, no knowledge of who I was.

Just a voice and a message.

I must dig it out and listen to it again.

Bits of it aligned beautifully with my life at that time—as if my present had been *shaped* by the echoes of the past.

I've had other moments of proof—communications or insights sent without the sender having any knowledge of my life or personality.
Just my name, my address, and a request.

I'll share those later, when I talk more about Hilltop Manor. There, I'll introduce you to the souls who stayed behind—to help our little Atom fulfill "His" purpose.

23

His lifeline remains ever open—with souls descending into Earthly life, and others ascending again to rest, before deciding their next earthly journey.

***

I had a thought the other day,
I saw existence in another way.
We sleep, we dream or so it would seem.
We wake, we breathe,
We find it hard to conceive
That a moment ago is now only a dream!

What I am trying to say
In an easier way
Is that night is the same as our wakening day
Or day is the same as that darkened sight!
It is all a dream!

This moment is real but the last has gone,
Alas it is true—
I could go on and on!
So dreams be reality forever more.
Yet dear friends, that might be a bore.
In the event of life seeming good
The dream could extend—
If only it could!
To continue the suffering would not be fair!
So dreams perhaps you had better stay
As night and day!

In our reality, we often look to those with great minds—those who have studied the deeper things we perhaps should have explored ourselves. There are so many souls who carry bits and pieces of the truth—the actual truth. If we dig deep enough, we eventually come to the center of that truth, and what do we find? *You. Us. We.* We are all truth because we exist. If we take the ego-centered "I" and place it within the name of Jesus, we arrive at *Je Suis*—French for "I am." *I am the way?* The Nazarene was supposedly one of the greatest spiritual teachers to have lived. In my opinion, he came to show us how to reach our spiritual goals. Sadly, his message has been misrepresented many times over the years. That said, I must admit I agree with certain things Mel Gibson has shared in his videos. He's another soul unafraid to speak out.

When we find our own pathway to spiritual discovery, I believe all positive things are acceptable. The things that uplift us are gifts. They help move us one step closer to the golden rung of the ladder that leads to spiritual freedom. We must listen to our inner emotions, because if we study them closely, they will often lead us to our own answers.

I believe that these great minds—those seeking truth—are simply listening. They aren't trying to control; they're trying to catapult the soul up the ladder. While I feel strongly that reincarnation is real, I've also come to believe that not every soul *has* to be reborn. It depends on whether or not we've completed the lessons we signed up for. Rebirth doesn't always happen right away after we leave this dimension.

My visual dreams are so vivid that I often see other people within them—clear as day. I once saw my husband dressed in a military uniform. Within the dream, I was knocking on the doors of old, quaint houses, many of which looked poor. I seemed to be collecting money—funnily enough, this was part of my actual job at the time. As I knocked, he walked toward me. We didn't acknowledge one another, but it was definitely him. Oddly, I once had the impression that he had been in jail. When I asked him, he laughed and told me it was true— he had been locked up while serving in the army! I hadn't known him then, and he'd never told me before. It gave me chills.

I've also seen darker images in my dreams. One time, I saw a friend being massacred by Native Americans. He was tied to a stake as arrows rained down on him. *Ouch!* It was graphic and shocking, but it felt like a memory.

Not every experience is pleasant. As I've said before, some are deeply frightening. Still, I believe having both the negative and the positive is a reflection of true free will.

Looking through my writings from way back in 1989, I came across the following entry...

I had a very intense astral dream last night. I, along with my usual gathering of friends, had spent an enjoyable evening beforehand at our usual haunt, "The Ship." I must admit to having had several alcoholic beverages. Also, in the light of certain events taking place, I sent out a special prayer before eventually falling asleep. I seemed to be happily wandering around. I wasn't at a party, and yet there was an air of celebration all around me.

I found myself watching four, five, maybe six young people performing very exact movements. It looked like dancing—but not the kind you see in a ballroom. It was more ritualistic, like a choreographed ceremony. Their timing was perfect. Then, suddenly, one of them stepped forward and reached into another's back. With precision, he removed the spinal column, along with part of the skull, and held it up for all to see. The one who had been "opened" didn't flinch, didn't scream. There was no pain—just solemnity. It was strangely beautiful, like watching a sacred rite from another world.

I must have been frightened by the whole experience. Someone told me I was next—that they were looking for me. And oh boy, did I run. I ran until I came across a soul who had already been through the process. She was calm. I questioned her, asked why it had to be done, and what it did to her. She said it was a great thing. But there was something in her eyes, something not quite right.

Soon, I was back at the scene. What I saw disturbed me deeply—souls stacked atop one another, groaning as if in pain. Each one of them had been "treated." Whatever it was, I didn't want it. I don't know what happened next. All I remember is feeling paralyzed—completely unable to move. I became aware of a faint light, as though coming through the bottom of my closed eyelids. I could hear someone fussing around me. I thought I was conscious, but something had happened in the sleep state, something powerful.

I tried with all my might to speak. I wanted to tell my mother that it was okay. But then something strange happened. I was crying out, "Ma! Ma!"—not with my voice, but with a voice inside me that wasn't mine. It was as though a baby was speaking through me. "I'm in here!" I cried. I wasn't just experiencing; I was witnessing. There seemed to be blood. My legs were bent, just as they would be during childbirth. I tried to straighten them. Then I heard someone say, "She doesn't realize that's how they should be."

I was aware, and yet I wasn't. I cried, but I didn't. I was in one *hell* of a state.

After a while, Sarah—my eldest daughter—seemed to appear around me. Then came Louise, my younger one, trying to give me a cigarette, thinking it would somehow help. (Smiles—trust her.) Someone nearby remarked, "If only she would be friendly."

At that time, I'd been trying to regress myself using a pendulum—a story I'll share in more detail later. I had hoped to reach back into the womb, and maybe beyond it into a past life. Did I succeed in this astral journey? Was reincarnation in motion?

And then again, I have to ask—was I on an alien ship?

You see, I don't disbelieve in aliens. Not in the least. In fact, I suspect they may be part of a higher authority. I once found myself on what I can only describe as the lower floor of a ship. My friends were with me, but I climbed onto a higher level, leaving them behind. I stepped into a room, and immediately I was overwhelmed by the sound—an intense, unrelenting noise of souls crying out. It was the sound of distress, of pleading for help and understanding.

I turned to one of the helpers and asked what it was. I was told, quite plainly, that those were the voices of souls in pain. Then, suddenly, the sound was shut off—just like that. Like a program had ended, the silence that followed was unnerving, almost more deafening than the cries had been. I didn't stay long.

***

On the **10th of June, 1989**, I wrote these words:

We are the light of the universe. All of mankind is one—each carrying the universal light within. Long ago, when we were still united as one consciousness, we made the decision to come to Earth and cleanse it. To uplift it, so it could reunite with its origin.

It's said the Earth was once divided from the sun. Was it due to a collision in the universe? Or something else entirely? Whatever the cause, the separation left the Earth in turmoil. Its magnetic energy dwindled, its surface cooled and solidified, and it began to deteriorate. It was as though the planet had been forgotten, left behind—until a divine scheme was formed.

Light was to be installed into heavier vessels—bodies—so it could remain tethered to Earth and begin healing it from within. In the beginning, we experimented with all sorts of vehicles. We gave them different names and different forms. But they were too heavy, too primitive. Over time, we phased them out. That's why so many species vanished—by intention, not accident.

Our mission is to one day leave all these vehicles behind, their remains nourishing the planet. And then, when the time is right, the Earth will be freed—lifted once again to return to the warmth of the sun.

If the wisdom of the world is blind to humankind, then maybe these bodies we walk in—our vehicles—really are of no consequence to the light within us. Maybe they exist only to enrich the planet while we live through them. If that's the case, then all our suffering, striving, and endless trial isn't meant to impress some divine scoreboard. It's simply the cleansing of the light inside us—scrubbing the soul clean through experience.

So perhaps, in the end, it's not the planet that needs saving. Perhaps Earth is just the ground we fall on until our light is ready to rise. Maybe when all light is uplifted—when each spark has rejoined the *Whole*—then the Earth, too, will serve its final purpose and be released. Or destroyed.

But there's a twist in the tale. That same light that once beamed down here has gotten used to this home. Disillusioned, distracted, and forgetful of the mission it came for. So it too must now be cleansed— right along with the planet.

I ended that piece with, *Ah, well, just thoughts. Food for thought.* Was it written from my subconscious? I believe that if we all tuned into our inner minds, we'd uncover so much more to think about. Just imagine if we all did this, then compared notes. We might even recognize ancient soul agreements, made before we left the safety of our original beginnings.

My husband, for example, always insisted there was no afterlife. Reincarnation, he believed, didn't exist. Spiritually, he was very grounded—he believed that when the body (our vehicle) passed on, it simply enriched the ground through burial. From that viewpoint, there was no spirit to continue, only matter returning to matter. And you know what? In some ways, that ties in with my earlier thoughts— surprising how much we can learn when we actually put all of our ideas on the table. He was never curious about the *whys* or *wherefores* of what happens after passing. His feet were firmly planted on the material level, and that's fair—after all, we *do* live in the material. But as I've said before, I believe it's wise to keep one foot in each world. To me, that's the key to understanding *why*. Why do some suffer while others seem spared? This is exactly where reincarnation and karma enter the picture for me.

As I go through my papers and writings from the past few decades, I've uncovered many OBEs. I'll share the more unusual ones as I go along. In the meantime, I recently came across a fascinating piece from April 7, 2019. It's from *Astral Physics and Timespace* (montalk.net) and titled "Research Notes." I haven't read it all—I prefer keeping things simple and letting myself acknowledge that these things just *happen.* Many people experience strange or powerful spiritual events, but they're afraid to speak up about them. I'm not. I prefer letting my subconscious speak first, and then I look for outside confirmation later. Forgive me if I repeat myself—*too many onions again! (smiles)*

What's surprising is that when I compare things I wrote many years ago to what I write today, the essence hasn't changed. My subconscious still orbits the same central theme: the planet and the afterlife.

Years ago, I perfected the use of a crystal pendulum. It "spoke" to me—on the material level, yes, but with wisdom that felt very spiritual. The pendulum would tell me a story, and then pick it up the next day like a long-lost friend continuing a conversation. Sometimes, it spun so quickly I could barely catch what it was saying. It was fascinating.

I also used the pendulum as a tool for self-hypnosis. It helped me sink into a deep, peaceful state where understanding could rise. I'd ask why something was bothering me, and it would show me the answer. My distress would dissolve. Still, I'd only recommend such practices under the guidance of someone reliable and sincere. Positive thoughts are essential.

For a while, the pendulum became my lifeline. I genuinely enjoyed its company.

It even gave me names and addresses connected to past lives— belonging to a few members of my family. I never followed up on them properly back then, though they certainly *sounded* authentic. Of course, the proof is always in the pudding, as they say. Maybe now that I've retrieved the information again, I'll have another look.

***

On September 20, 1988, I wrote this curious little piece:

It came about within a dream, where things were not as they would seem. I found myself at a gathering—laughing gaily, caught up in the joy around me. There was a feeling of celebration in the air, though the clothing didn't seem from the present day. Nor did it clearly belong to any other time. I was simply there. I sat with two loved ones. Among the crowd, I noticed a peculiar figure—a person who seemed almost like a scarecrow. At first, as he bent over, I thought the seam of his trousers had split and that his bottom was bare. I got the impression he didn't much care about whether he was clean or not.

He kept standing upright and then bending again. One leg up, one leg down—moving like a jester, or a clown, arms swinging in odd rhythm with his legs. I can still see it clearly, but it's difficult to capture the surreal nature of the scene in words. His clothing was ragged and careless, but it was his face—or lack thereof struck me the most.

He had no visible face. Instead, his head appeared to be enclosed in a cage, as if meant to hold the skull together. Where a face should have been, there were only maggots. Yet, he danced on—happily, even joyfully—completely unaware of his grotesque condition, lost in his own world, surrounded by strangers.

I didn't want him to see me. I feared how I might react if I came face-to-face with such a haunting image of death. And yet—he was happy.

Reading this now, I can't help but wonder: was this soul at the moment of death? Had he realized he was no longer bound to a suffering body? Had he stepped into his true self—his spirit—leaving behind the consequences of his misdeeds? The image reminded me of the old punishment of locking criminals in cages, left exposed to the elements and the birds. As always, after such vivid experiences, I tried to record them as quickly as possible. Some, like this one, still make for very curious and thought-provoking reading.

***

On September 21, 1988, I wrote:

Visions of the past are like reflections on a glass.

In my astral dream last night, I saw myself within a face as black as night. The mirror was clear, and I felt no fear. This face looked back at me, calm and without menace. At one point, I had the impression that the front of my hair was strikingly white. The face itself did not appear aged. I vaguely recall the possibility of a hat upon my head, and I remember seeing strands of hair in green tones. Of course, in these dreams, things are not always as they seem. Still, I wonder—was this another life?

I also had a beautiful out-of-body experience. I even felt my astral body lift out. As I lay in bed alone, it felt as if someone were cuddling me. Gradually, I became aware that the bodies were separating. Though my eyes were closed, I could still see. I saw the clouds as I drifted out through the wall behind my bed. I knew then: I was tripping.

Soon after, I was walking happily along a beach. Even then, I remained conscious of my physical body still lying in bed. I had a silly cough and was determined not to let it ruin the trip. I focused and managed to stay on the beach. I remember thinking to myself, *I am spirit*. With that thought, I tried to fly—but I couldn't lift off the ground. I suppose some part of this human vehicle still whispered to me that I was a mere mortal.

Then, a blurred light appeared, moving toward me. As it cleared, I became aware of a young man dressed in white. Upon his back rested a set of wings. Laugh if you wish, my loving ones, but it was a lovely sight. I have previously written about a time when helpers seemed to be removing wings from my own back. Bearing that in mind, I now wonder—was this soul another astral traveler, watching over me? Or was "he" an angel from a higher realm? I had written "young man," but more recent experiences are making me reconsider. A few months ago, I awoke to see an angel standing by my bed. "He" had tightly cropped, wavy hair and a deeply calming presence.

On November 23, 1989, I wrote about a dream that deeply unsettled me. I remember the fear I felt at the thought of losing those

I love to a heavenly choir "stationed above." I awoke with tears on my mind, simply hoping that destiny would be kind. As I've said before, not every experience is comforting—especially those involving loved ones. Some were quite frightening.

I had also introduced my pendulum a few pages back. I used to write down as much as I could after using it. On one occasion, I wrote: *My pendulum has been trying its hardest to spell out a word that I know I've heard before. My mind wouldn't let it flow in a particular vein. The material world pulled it back down again.* I had the sense that it was a Latin word, one that many might know—but I, admittedly, was no scholar.

Then something quite amazing happened. I received a selection of books and followed instructions in a particular section discussing the art of *bibliomancy*—the practice of reading the first word or phrase that appears when a book falls open at random. The idea is that the word holds guidance or meaning, especially when it appears without a question being asked. I know some may debate such practices, but I believe in trial and error when it comes to the spirit. Bibliomancy, in essence, is gaining spiritual insight through the written word.

Being me, I loved the idea of experimenting. I decided to give it a try—eyes closed tight, holding the book like a true believer. I let the pages fall where they pleased, pointed my finger, and peeked. I'm sure I looked a bit silly, but to my surprise, I read the words: *Tempvs Omnia et singvla consvmens.* That Latin word my pendulum had been struggling to spell was *Omnia.* I hadn't known at the time, but it meant "all." The full phrase: "Time devours all and each."

I strongly believe the pendulum had tapped into my subconscious. It had been giving me answers, just as bibliomancy seemed to. Perhaps the two are simply different ways of tuning in. As I said, trial and error is the way to discover what works. I've used both methods many times, always with a curious and open heart.

*****

Chapter 4

Life is a difficult thing to define. We all carry different ideas about the whys and wherefores. What I've come to believe is that while we live in the material world, we're also capable of tapping into the etheric layer of our being. Many will understand what I mean. Others may be confused. But at the heart of it, it all boils down to one word: faith. Faith in oneself. Faith in the unknown. The real question is—are we truly alone?

***

Through my own trials and tribulations, I was guided toward a path. I followed it. I walked it. And in my book *Heaven to Earth*, I explain how I came to use prayer—perhaps selfishly at times, but always sincerely. I did things my way, and I remain deeply grateful for the blessings I received.

Many years ago, I joined the Spiritualist Church. In the beginning, I was flooded with knowledge—things I had never realized were inherent to the human condition. I will always be thankful for what I learned. It was proof in action.

But in time, I had to walk away.

The reason? Hypocrisy. The moment I joined the committee, I realized that everything depended on being part of the inner circle. You were "in" if you aligned with the favored few. The president once asked me outright whose side I was on. I remember thinking—why must there be sides at all? Aren't we all seekers? Isn't that the very reason we came?

Even worse, I discovered that a few members were being turned away because of their sexuality. I was told flat out that if I had been gay, I wouldn't have been accepted. That shattered something in me. I was trying to be kind, open, and supportive of all souls—because surely, truth seekers come in all forms. We travel in many vehicles.

Despite that disappointment, my awakening during that period was profound. I joined a development circle. At first, I felt so out of place. I used to sit there thinking, *What on earth am I doing here?* I was just me. Ordinary. No special powers. No revelations. Just a soul, trying to be part of the greater Whole.

And that, I believe, is what we're all striving toward—unity with something greater, even if we don't consciously know it.

Little by little, I began to tune in. I started sensing something that had always been there but unnoticed. I felt connected to a force beyond myself. It was beautiful. It was humbling.

The Church, for all its flaws, brought in some incredible people. Many mediums gave sincere and meaningful messages. Of course, some were just chasing applause, seeking glory. That old, tired story of ego and false hope. But others—others were real.

One of the most remarkable sessions I witnessed featured a Transfiguration Medium. She was extraordinary. The Church was packed that night—too packed, if we're honest, for safety. Even my husband agreed to come. It was his first encounter with the unknown, though he always supported my spiritual interests. His passions were... of a different kind (smiles). He enjoyed a good drink, and we shared many lovely nights out, dancing and sipping. But this was something else entirely.

He sat, bemused, watching the proceedings unfold.

The medium began projecting spirit. Messages were delivered— claimed by those they resonated with. Faces formed beside hers: some with spectacles, others with moustaches. It was fascinating. The detail, the clarity—it all felt incredibly real.

Then came a spirit who spoke of things closely tied to my husband. Markets. Specific references that, to me, pointed clearly to his grandmother. His mother had once run a stall in the marketplace. The signs were there.

But he wouldn't claim it.

Several others tried to take the message, but the medium gently turned them away. It wasn't theirs. I hoped my husband would step forward, just this once. But no. And then the spirit face simply faded.

It was a missed opportunity. And I didn't feel it was my place to intervene.

Eventually, after several moving connections, the medium stepped back. Then, a towering figure appeared—a Native American spirit guide, complete with a long headdress that flowed down his back. The ectoplasm that formed him was almost luminous. It was stunning to witness.

When the evening ended, the medium stood at the top of the stairs, shaking hands with everyone as they left. My dear husband, in all his worldly charm, took her hand and said, "A good show!" (*smiles*). He didn't believe a word of it, but at least he showed up. And sometimes, that's enough.

Later, we attended another session with a different transfiguration medium. Sadly, it was disappointing. The first medium had set such a high bar that no one else could quite measure up.

I could share many stories. But more than anything, my hope is to give peace to those who find themselves in a state of confusion. To help them realize—we all hold our own answers. We are not just who we appear to be. While I can't claim to solve the mystery of reincarnation, I do believe anything is possible. As I've said before, in my opinion, we are spirit, simply occupying heavy vehicles that anchor us to a material earth.

It's up to each of us, in our own time and way, to seek. There are always doors waiting. We just have to knock on the right one. Sometimes that may take several lifetimes. Who knows, eh?

***

I've participated in many circles and meditation groups over the years—and if you ask me, meditation is the key to opening the inner spirit. At one point, I truly believed I had grounded myself. But as it turns out, life had more to show me.

One evening, Rob (my husband) and I were at our local pub, sitting near the main entrance. As the door opened and two customers walked in, I saw—just at the edge of my vision—two spiritual "helpers" behind them. Each helper reflected a different culture. I felt a jolt of excitement. I had never experienced anything like that outside of a circle.

As we sat there watching the darts team, I had a strong impression of the Salvation Army. It seemed to be connected to one of the players. When that player went to the bar, I followed and stood nearby. I didn't want to blurt out what I was sensing, so I eased into it and asked if she had any connection to the SA.

She said, "No."

So, I dropped it.

Then she added, "Well, my mother was."

That opened the door.

I told her I believed her mother was there with her. She looked surprised. I walked back to my seat, quietly impressed. This was the first time I had experienced spirit communication outside of a spiritualist setting.

As I continued to watch the match, the phrase *"Come into the Garden, Maud"* echoed in my mind. I laughed to myself. There was no way I was going to march over and ask if her mother's name was Maud—she'd think I was completely mad!

The next day, during work (I used to call on customers to collect their weekly payments), I visited a friend who also happened to be one of the darts players. She told me her friend had been quite moved by what I'd said the night before. That meant a lot to me. It was another small piece of proof—evidence of the soul's separation, and its connection to the Infinite.

I casually asked her, "By the way, what was her mother's name?"

She smiled and replied, "Maud."

I could have gone back that night and asked. But let's be honest—many people, myself included, hesitate to share their experiences for fear of ridicule. I've learned to test the waters gently first.

***

Sometimes we have to trust our deepest instincts. Our subconscious may hold hidden truths that our conscious minds have forgotten. If we can learn to tune into that deeper part of ourselves, we might just find we're closer to our original purpose—the one we agreed upon before descending the golden lifeline.

***

As I've mentioned before, my pendulum became a lifeline to me. It felt like an extension of myself—something just outside the physical body but deeply connected. Every evening, I'd tune in. I'd sit with it for hours, soaking in the messages it gave. Many of them lined up perfectly with what was happening in my life. Sometimes it even used words I wasn't familiar with—words I never used in my own speech.

One evening after a long session, I sat on the edge of my bed. Suddenly, I felt as if someone was breathing into my nostrils. It reminded me of the phrase *"Breathe on me, breath of God."* I didn't resist. I simply let it happen.

Then I lay down, fully aware of everything going on. I watched the clock on my wall. And in that moment, I was aware of being in three places at once. In each place, I was experiencing something completely distinct. I saw my friend's face and chatted with her. In another corner of the room, a booming voice was speaking. I didn't panic. I just listened. It was all so vivid, so real. I remember thinking, *Now I know how to do this!*

I could see the clock the entire time. I was conscious. Present. And yet simultaneously, I was elsewhere. It's an experience I've never forgotten—never quite replicated to that degree again.

***

Another time, I was watching an old black-and-white film. The kind where people still traveled by horse and cart. As I watched a cart roll down the road, I suddenly *was* there—sitting behind it, inside the film itself. I know I was fully focused on the screen, but my soul? It was somewhere else entirely.

It made me wonder: can we transfer our soul into other vehicles, other times, at will?

There is so much we still don't understand.

At a previous home, Rob had built a small fishpond in our front garden. Someone gifted us a very large goldfish that had been kept in a small bowl for years. The poor little soul was so pale, we weren't even sure it would survive. Still, we gently released it into the pond, hopeful. I really wanted that fish to live.

After my experience with the horse and cart, I thought, *Why not try giving it healing?* So I did. And just for a fleeting moment—I was inside the fish.

The thing to remember is that each experiment like that takes a lot of energy. Willpower. Focus. Our daily responsibilities don't just vanish so we can go floating around the ether. These tasks ask for discipline—and surrender.

But when they work—when there's even the slightest result—it's incredibly uplifting.

***

One of the most personal and beautiful moments I've ever experienced came when my father died unexpectedly. I was lying on my bed when a strange vibration began at my feet. I stayed still, just observing. Slowly, I drifted into what seemed like a sleep state.

Then I opened my eyes.

And there he was. My father's face was right in front of mine. He was wearing his thick-rimmed glasses. He was smiling.

"Cheerio then," he said.

And just like that—he was gone.

He had come to say goodbye before continuing on. Bless his cotton socks. The first man in my life had passed. He was a good man. Gentle. A peacemaker. A devoted husband and a brilliant father.

He'd only spent a short time in the hospital before passing. My family and I had gone to see him. I remember sitting with him as he stared off into the distance. He didn't say much, but then he turned to me and said, "I'll be alright."

I thought he meant he'd recover.

But he passed that night. A few days later, he visited me. It was a sad time for all of us, especially my mother.

***

Not long after my father passed, I lost my daughter, Louise.

I was sitting on the settee, watching television, when suddenly I shifted into another level of being. I wasn't trying. It just happened. I became aware of a small hand.

It was Louise's.

I could sense someone on her side of the veil guiding her. At the same time, someone was guiding me. We reached toward each other and held hands. That was all—just her little hand in mine.

When I returned to full consciousness, I realized I'd been holding the TV remote. I just sat there afterward, quietly savoring the moment. It wasn't wishful thinking. I *know* these things happen. I was lucky— truly blessed—to be the recipient of such a visit. Louise hadn't even been on my mind at the time.

Bless her.

***

I believe that in the sleep state, we visit our loved ones who have passed on. I also believe healing is done by caring family members—on both sides of the veil.

***

Before my father-in-law, Harold, passed away from cancer, I had a strange experience at the library. I was browsing books when my hand landed on one that seemed to give off an enormous wave of energy. Intrigued, I opened it.

It was a book on color healing.

I studied it intensely and put myself into a spiritual state of mind. As I focused on Harold—following the instructions—I received a clear message through the mind: he had been taken to the hospital.

Not long after that, the tumor disappeared. He was given another chance at life.

But Harold was a heavy smoker. In time, the illness returned.

He was a very down-to-earth man, unlikely to believe anything too mystical. But I do. I believe in healing. In faith. But I also believe we have to work *with* it. Healing isn't something we just receive—it's something we must cooperate with.

***

To me, we *are* free—we just keep ourselves tied to this material plane. When we feel troubled, if we can reach out with open minds and hearts, and find the kind of faith that uplifts rather than confines, we may begin to understand our purpose more clearly. In time, we start to realize our own unique goals of understanding. We must feel it for ourselves. Other people's truths aren't always ours to carry—each one of us walks a different path.

But be wary of those who claim *their* truth is *the* truth. There are forces that will mislead us—without question. And once we're off track, it's not always easy to find our way back to that yellow brick road that leads us home. Sometimes, we have to weather the storm just to be lowered gently into the arms of understanding... into our original beginnings.

***

My son Stephen was born with a hole in his heart. At just five years old, he had to undergo surgery to repair it. I never spoke to my children about anything spiritual or metaphysical—not back then. I let them grow into their own sense of belief, never forcing church or doctrine onto them.

One day, a few years after his operation, Stephen quietly told me about a dream he'd had. We were staying at my parents' house in Exeter, Devon. He said he saw soldiers fighting in the sitting room of the house, no less. There was gunfire, and Stephen said he had been hit in the heart.

He told me this with complete innocence and certainty. "That's why I had the hole," he said, very matter-of-factly.

It intrigued me so much that I began investigating the history of the area. My parents' house sat right on the outskirts of the old City Wall. I have no doubt that battles were fought right on that very ground.

I've since watched several documentaries on children remembering past lives. It's intriguing—but I can imagine how worrying it must be for the parents. The innocence of children—before they're influenced or silenced by the world—is something sacred.

***

I've been leafing through an old diary of mine, full of notes and jottings from 1977 and earlier. While not related to reincarnation, I found this little piece tucked inside. Just for fun, really:

The Children's Party

Three little children, hail and hearty,
All dressed up to go to a party.
One fell down and that left two,
Two little children, hail and hearty,
Both dressed up to go to a party,
One fell asleep and that left one,
One all alone, not quite as hearty,
Not so keen to go to the party,
So they all stayed home.

*****

Chapter 5:
Hilltop Manor

Let me introduce you to *Hilltop Manor*—a place that revealed itself to me during my pendulum dreams. As I may have mentioned, each evening I would sit quietly and allow the pendulum to speak to me. Each session continued a story from the night before, unfolding little by little, as if the tale had its own consciousness. One such narrative revolved around a cousin of mine who tragically drowned at sea. His body was never recovered.

His mother, my aunt, was a woman of formidable character. She had a strong, almost overpowering personality. My cousin, by contrast, seemed to be timid, gentle, and often overwhelmed by her strength. Despite this, he had a boat which he would take out on the water with his friends, as well as a couple of parents and their child. One day, something went terribly wrong. They were all lost at sea. Only the mother and the child were eventually found along the coastline. The boat itself was recovered, but my cousin and the others were gone.

What troubled many of us was that my cousin was known to be a strong swimmer. In fact, just a couple of months before the accident, he had saved my brother from drowning during a family holiday. His disappearance left many questions behind, and the sorrow of it lingered for years.

At the time of his passing, I was nearing my 18th birthday. I had only recently met him. He was part of my Welsh family, and due to the distance and the era we lived in, we rarely saw our extended family from Wales. Yet, in that short time, I grew very fond of him. After the accident, I found myself compelled to write. The words came quickly, unfiltered, pouring out from that deep well of emotion that only grief can summon.

Lionel

It never should have been, my love,
It never should have been.
Of boats and sea and fun, my love,
I know you were so keen.
Had you stayed at home, my love,
Had you stayed at home—
It never would have been, my love,
It never would have been.
Rest in peace, dear cousin. Rest in peace.

At the time, I remember my mother and I both wondering if my cousin had somehow survived and simply couldn't face the family, knowing the others had been lost. It was such a painful time, as no one could say for certain what had actually happened. We could only guess. Around that same time, another cousin—this one from our Australian side of the family—also disappeared. Her family was distraught. What made things more curious was that my pendulum began telling me that the two cousins were together in Australia.

The pendulum continued with different elements of this story, night after night. There was no logical reason for them to have been together. Our family was very divided by distance, and I doubt they even knew one another. There was nothing in our family history that would suggest a link. Was my subconscious trying to tell me something? Or was it just playing tricks on my mind? Even now, I feel the pendulum was tuning into something deeper within me—a part of myself we are all capable of touching if we try. How do we ever really know? Trial and error, I suppose.

I never followed up on it. My aunt had already suffered more than enough—he was her only son. So instead of probing further, I wrote down my pendulum dreams in a notebook. The words came so fast, almost automatically.

There was one evening in particular when I woke up with words racing through my mind so quickly I could hardly catch them. It felt like poetry, and it flowed from the dream state, not through conscious concentration. That was how, over time, *Hilltop Manor* was introduced to me.

So take a little walk with me now. Surround yourself in peace and understanding. Visualize—because that's such an important part of this. Imagine yourself walking, or floating, along whatever type of pathway you choose. I often visualize clouds, because the Manor exists somewhere between Heaven and Earth. It rests on a hilltop. It's a place where you can realize your dreams, where you can face your troubles. It's a place where our helpers from the spirit come to greet us and guide us. I walk, or float, upon a clouded path. Alongside me is Ellie, my spiritual elephant. On her back sits Samid.

Samid came into my life through a developing circle, during meditation and visualization. I've written before about that Church circle. While sitting with a few friends, I had written to a psychic. I simply gave her my name and address, along with a request: could she send me a picture of someone who might be with me in spirit?

I wrote to her four times—and each time I received something meaningful in return.

The first response came after our "leader"—for lack of a better word—told me during one circle that I had a Sister of Mercy with me. I asked him if he knew her name. He said no. In my mind, I immediately heard the name "Theresa." I left it at that. Then the first picture arrived. It was of a sister, and underneath her portrait was the name: *Theresa*. At the time, I was so new to all this—it both intrigued and thrilled me. Along with the portrait came a beautiful message. Part of it declared that Theresa was a guide of peace and love. She brought radiant healing energies. There was more, but that part felt quite personal. I saw her with young children in my mind—she truly was a spiritual mother.

So pleased with that result, I wrote for more. The next portrait I received was "Jamahal"—an Indian spirit of great wisdom. According to the note, his radiance brings peaceful and beautiful vibrations. Later, the leader of our circle gave someone else that same name as one of their guides. In my excitement, I interrupted and said, "No, he is with me," and then explained about the portrait I had received. I doubt I was very popular in that moment—but I had to be honest (smiles).

The third portrait I received was of *Samid*, a Persian guide of peace and love. The accompanying introduction described him as being connected to teachers of spiritual truths. Reading that paper again now, I see it mentioned that the color orange is associated with the strength of mind power.

He comes as a silent, loving influence. I once had a vision of myself sitting on a Persian carpet—this was before I even met Samid. Still, I often felt his energy around me.

The last portrait I received was of Doctor Borg Christenson, a Swedish healing entity. At that time—back in my forties—I was praying for healing for my daughter, Louise, who had dislocated hips. Her story is shared in my book *Heaven to Earth*.

I believe I applied for one more portrait, but, unfortunately, it was lost in the post. The one I would have especially liked was of my Indian helper with his long, majestic headdress. I experienced his presence many times. The most vivid was during a particular circle session when the group's head—our "master"—came in and began moaning about his day. Personally, I believe there's a time and place for everything, but back then, I was a bit more timid. I wasn't one to say "boo to a goose" (*smiles*). I was very focused, though. I was genuinely invested in the circle's purpose and my own search for spiritual teachings.

Our circle was made up of many different personalities. Some just wanted to offload their problems. Others didn't seem to see the point of the things we were experiencing. That night, I softly commented that perhaps the "master" shouldn't bring his daily worries into the sacred space of the circle. A hush fell over the room. One of the other girls quickly reprimanded me. It wasn't well received.

To balance the energy, I quietly concentrated on the "master," sending out healing thoughts. I sensed an energy around me—gentle, yet powerful. Suddenly, the "master" stopped speaking and turned toward me. He asked if I realized who was present. I did, of course. But having all eyes on me made me feel awkward. Still, it confirmed something I'd long suspected: he genuinely saw the energies around us.

That evening, the circle collapsed. But it was also the first moment I felt a deep trust in the evidence I was receiving. On my walk home, I ran my hand through my hair and found a young feather tucked in it. I had washed my hair before sitting, so I knew it hadn't been there earlier. My helper—later named "Hawke" by another medium—had made his presence known. Unfortunately, two members of the circle didn't appreciate it. Faith is essential in this kind of work. But unless one understands the spiritual protocol, it's difficult to follow and interpret the signs being given.

Looking back, I believe circles should have been divided into two groups: one for those simply seeking comfort and another for those who genuinely wished to learn and grow spiritually. At the same time, I recognize that many troubled souls walk this earth—and every soul deserves to be heard and supported. That's just my opinion, of course. Everything was still relatively new to me back then, and there were certainly moments when I handled things poorly. We all have times when we just want to fit in—so we bite our tongues and avoid making waves.

But unless you're sitting with the right people, the purpose of circles gets lost. Without unity of purpose, we can't generate the kind of energy that helps us understand the infinite. To truly grow, we must work as one. I firmly believe that many "Helpers" remained behind with our little Atom. They stay to guide the souls who have chosen to enter the earthly schoolrooms for deeper lessons.

As I've said before, there's a belief that we don't *have* to be reborn. Personally, I know that if I want to reach out to my Helpers, they'll be there—as long as I'm willing to listen (*smiles*).

Now, with "Hawke," I once decided to experiment. I took a photograph of myself—taking a photograph. I stood in front of the bathroom mirror, lights off, camera in hand. I entered a meditative state, then clicked the shutter. In those days, we used film, and when I had it developed, what I saw stunned me. There I was, but around my head was a faint but undeniable headdress. It had nothing to do with reflections or shadows. It was simply there.

I've introduced you to my "Helpers." Rightly or wrongly, I accept them. At times, I feel I've let them down. But let's continue our journey to the Manor. I walk—or sometimes float—with Ellie and Samid. If you prefer another companion, then visualize them. Let the imagination lead.

Inside Hilltop Manor, there are all sorts of rooms where one can sit and meditate. There are books of understanding—just think of one. Search for it. Close your eyes and visualize the words as they come to life. See how you feel as each word makes its presence known. Don't worry if none of it seems to make sense at first. Often, we are our own worst enemies. Write the words down. Let your inner mind flow; it will know exactly where to go.

If you're feeling troubled, sit quietly and ask for help. Close your eyes. Relax your body from the feet upward. Pay attention to how your solar plexus feels. Speak gently to yourself. Steady your thoughts. Try to focus on something positive. And if you can't, then ask yourself why. What's really troubling you? Talk it over in your mind. Consider what you *can* fix in this world—and what you simply cannot. Leave the burdens you cannot carry behind, and surround them in a soft blue healing light. What do they say? "Let go and let God." Or as the scripture offers, "Seek and ye shall find."

One of the rooms inside the Manor houses the Akashic Records. These are said to contain all our past lives. According to Wikipedia, the Records are "a compendium of all universal events, thoughts, words, emotions, and intent ever to have occurred in the past, present, and future." Of course, there's no scientific proof they exist. But with a bit of imagination and focused visualization, we can sit quietly, empty our minds of worry, and enter that sacred space. Think of something meaningful. Picture yourself flipping through those ancient pages. Let your inner eye form the images. Watch what comes. Visualizing is part and parcel of the journey.

Wander through the Manor, and you'll find whatever room you need to help you with life's lessons. Step through a door and you may find yourself in a beautiful courtyard, where a tranquil pond sits encircled by ornamental brickwork. Let your imagination color the scene—clear healing waters shimmering with possibility. In my vision, this pond contains a mix of waters, including droplets of the sacred healing liquid from Lourdes. Just for fun, imagine everyone returning from their own spiritual trips, pouring small bottles of Lourdes water into this single pond at Hilltop Manor.

I once had a visual dream where I took my three children to Lourdes:

I had a dream so pure and sweet,
My heart was there my joy complete.
My soul was saved.
O little ones you came with me
We bathed in waters cool and free.
Your souls were saved.
Together we prayed
Then saw the light.
The joys we shared having won the fight.
Our souls were saved.

***

Find a room to meditate in. Bring along a friend or even a few. Create a circle—the energy you generate together will help. Make sure the space is filled with positive vibes. As you sit together, concentrate on one another and take note of your solar plexus. (For context, the solar plexus is the third chakra in the body, situated just above the belly button.) According to various sources, it's associated with personal power. Over the years, I've come to believe we can recognize a situation just by tuning into its vibration.

Some years ago, my husband Rob and I went on a cruise that took us to Jerusalem. We walked along a narrow street that led to what is believed to be the resting place of the Nazarene's story. Inside the building, on a lower floor, was a kind of enclosure with a sculpted head of the figure. People quietly filed past to pay their respects and offer thanks.

Up and on the next level, there was a raised platform behind a barrier. A cut-out section allowed one or two people to look down and watch those below. It was a small space—barely enough for two or three people. The room itself was plain, and Rob and I were the only ones there at the time. I stepped behind the cut-out section, and immediately, I was overwhelmed. The emotions—the vibrations— were intense. I felt tears, but they didn't feel like mine. They were the tears of all those who had stood in that space before me. I moved to the center of the room, and the feeling passed. When I stepped back into that same spot again, it returned. I now believe it was my solar plexus responding—picking up the emotional residue of others.

Over time, I've come to understand that not all feelings we carry are our own. Sometimes they belong to someone else we're close to or empathizing with. That's where things can get tricky. We must learn to tell the difference. If you're feeling low, stop and ask yourself— why? Try to test your solar plexus. It's always trial and error, just like when I tried tuning into the elderly gentleman (a helper) who mentioned 1945.

Back to the idea of forming circles—I once hosted one at home. I placed Tarot cards in the center. Each person was invited to select a card, and after the circle was complete, I would read its meaning to them. Every single time, the card resonated deeply. One sitter even found herself connecting with a loved one in spirit.

Always surround your circle with blue healing light. Ask for love, understanding, and clarity. Just as a building gathers the energy within it, Hilltop Manor can hold your energy too. Visualize it being filled with positivity. There's nothing to fear.

Hilltop Manor will remain as long as you want it to. Visit it often—I do (smiles). Visualize your Helpers. I truly believe we are never alone, no matter what.

Each experience I've shared, to me, shows that the spirit—or soul—is capable of separating from the material aspect of life. Spirit finds ways to show itself, in one form or another.

For example, when Rob and I were looking for our first mobile caravan, I was standing outside by the car, wondering where we might go to find one. Suddenly, a voice—outside of myself—gave me an address. It was loud and clear. Curious, I bought a magazine on caravans later that day. Sure enough, the place mentioned by the voice was advertised right there in the pages! It was quite far from where we lived, so we didn't go, but we found a site closer instead. Still, it left quite an impression.

Over the years, a friend of mine introduced me to the Ouija board. I have to admit, I wasn't entirely comfortable sitting with her—most of her questions were about how much money her mother had (smiles). In contrast, my first question was: "How did the planet come about?" The answer I received was: "By fire."

Later, when my mother came to stay with us, we sat down to try the board together. My mother was a strong-willed but gentle woman. Very capable. She ran a good home and always kept a proper table. Every Saturday, she'd cook and rope me into peeling cooking apples—ugh, I can still taste them! She always helped when she visited.

That day, we sat with the board, and my mother asked about her own mother, who was quite ill at the time. The board told her that my grandmother was with one of her brothers. It explained a few things that made sense to my mother. When she called her brother in Wales, he told her exactly what the board had already said.

To be honest, I think we should be cautious. It's just like learning to drive a car—if abused, it can be dangerous. But on the other hand, it can be a great source of comfort. Once again, I wonder: does it tap into our subconscious? It definitely seems to work with the right vibrations.

I once heard that if a child is born but does not live, its spirit continues its journey in the higher realms of light. I had a miscarriage a long time ago. Out of curiosity, I decided to ask the board about it. I was told that it had been a boy. I asked for his name and was told it was "Burt." When I asked who had named him, I was told that I had—while in the sleep state. That struck a chord with me. My father was named Albert, often called Bert. At the time, I remember thinking that "Burt" with a "u" felt like a more modern version. It felt meaningful. Perhaps a coincidence, perhaps not.

I never really disown anything. I always keep an open mind, because at the end of the day—as we all know—we simply do not know.

One lovely experience happened before my daughter became pregnant. I was resting on my settee, and Sarah was sitting in a chair opposite me. I must have dozed off, because when I opened my eyes, I saw a little girl standing over Sarah's head. Her hair was dark blonde, tied with small blue ribbons.

I watched her in amazement. Slowly, she began to disappear—from her shoulders to her head—until only her eyes and forehead remained. Then, she vanished… just like that.

When Sarah gave birth to her first child, I felt so sure it would be a little girl. But it wasn't. A little boy arrived, and sadly, he didn't stay. Later, we welcomed Luke. And eventually, Melanie was born—a lovely lass in every way.

When Mel was about two or three years old, we attended a family wedding. I was seated at the top table. As I sat there, Mel came up to me, just tall enough that only the top of her head and her eyes were visible above the table. I stared at her in wonder. That was the child I had seen all those years earlier. I took a photograph to remember the moment. These things do happen. Had that little soul descended the ladder of rebirth to make her home with us? I believe so.

Though I haven't had any significant visual dreams lately, I did have an out-of-body experience just a few weeks ago. I had been waiting for a book to arrive. The sender had promised to email me when it was posted. In the early hours of one fine morning, I thought I heard a knock at the front door. I found myself shouting, "Okay, I'm coming!" I thought it must be the postman with the book.

As I descended the stairs—in what I now believe was an astral state—I had a vision of myself opening the door. The postman was standing there holding two parcels, one longer than the other. Then the image faded, and I returned to sleep. When I woke up, the experience was still vivid in my mind. I told my granddaughter's partner about it, just to confirm no one had actually been at the door. He said no—no one had knocked.

A day or two later, I received an email saying the book had been posted. When it arrived, there was only one parcel—the smaller one. A few days after that, the longer one appeared. I truly believe my enthusiasm took my astral body out of the physical in anticipation of the delivery. My spirit went ahead, then returned to the body so I could continue sleeping.

***

I often wonder: how many of our ancestors have climbed and descended those strings of gold? Strings that eventually became a golden ladder of hope. If reincarnation is real, it's not such a stretch to think that we may even be our own ancestors. In this lifetime, anything is possible. On the other hand, perhaps we're playing out the karma of those who came before us.

When I lost my parents in 1999, I found, among their papers, a partially completed family tree my mother had started. There wasn't much on it, but it was a beginning. I had also purchased a book that contained some Abdey family history, complete with names and addresses. The surname itself was easier to track than something common like "Smith," so I wrote to everyone listed in that book. Gradually, my own lineage began to grow. I made many friends along the way, each helping the other in small but meaningful ways.

The story, as it's told, is that the name began in Wath Upon Dearne when two cousins named Brown took over Abdy Farm. They began referring to themselves as "Brown de Abdy," eventually dropping the "de." We know, of course, that "de" means "of." It's said that "Abdy" means "dwellers by the Abbey." Personally, I have a feeling that the name might have its roots in France or Germany. In older times, records were often misread, and as a result, "Abdy" became "Addy" in some branches. Wath had families with both spellings. My own family line added a twist—we became "Abdey."

There's so much to share about this journey. Genealogy, as a hobby, is far easier now than it was in years past. Thanks to the diligence of one particularly passionate Abdey researcher, the family name was traced all the way back to 1345. I, along with others, have since been able to build upon that foundation. It's a fascinating tree filled with many notable names—famous or otherwise—each playing out their destinies in their own unique ways.

Each time a link is found, there's a wonderful sense of satisfaction. With others, I've built several branches of the surname. It's my belief that, in time, they'll all meld into the same 1345 tree, completing the picture. The very idea that we can unite our minds here on earth—pooling our energy and insight—makes me feel hopeful. Imagine if we could all just lift our thoughts together, allowing our subconscious to guide us. Could we then, perhaps, unite with the infinite?

I can wholeheartedly recommend genealogical research as a healing tool. It has helped me tremendously. And you might find a few surprises along the way—eye-openers that change the way you see your own story. As we explore our ancestral past, we begin to understand the deeper meaning behind "Judge not, lest ye be judged." We might discover our own family has its fair share of black sheep. That, too, is part of the journey.

Most libraries offer research facilities, and of course, today's online resources are immense. DNA testing, too, can reveal new branches and clues, connecting people across continents. My first major breakthrough was discovering the twin brother of my great-grandfather. After exchanging a few letters, I received a photograph of another brother. To complete my joy, I realized I already had a photo of both men standing next to my grandfather at one of his sibling's weddings. Along the way, I discovered family connections in America, Canada, Australia, and across the UK.

I often wonder how many of our ancestors chose to remain in the heavens alongside our Atom. How many descended that golden ladder once again to be reborn? It's strange to think that they might still be with us—just in different forms. Could that explain déjà vu? As we know, the phrase is French and means "already seen." How many times have we walked into a building that felt eerily familiar? A house that stirred something deep in the soul—had we once lived there in another life?

There are so many possibilities. Sometimes when I'm driving down a winding country lane, I imagine a highwayman riding along—cloak billowing, hat tipped, pistol in hand. It all seems oddly familiar. Could I have been a highwayman? (Big smiles.) Those who study reincarnation often suggest visualizing the thing you admire most.

Ask yourself: What are you drawn to? What do you love more than anything—and why?

Think about it. Take it a step further. Imagine being a part of that world. Have you ever watched a television show and suddenly felt it physically—someone squeezing lemons and your teeth cringe from the imagined bitterness? Or you catch a scent you can't actually smell, but somehow it's there in your mind? You might say it can't be done—but I believe it can. With a bit of practice, it becomes second nature. We already feel the tears and the laughter in movies or books. So why not take it further?

Hypnotism is one way of reaching the inner mind. It can open doors to understanding and bring forth answers we otherwise might not see. At one point in my life, I self-hypnotized to work through a personal problem. I placed myself into a meditative state, and upon awakening, the answer came to me clearly. The issue, remarkably, disappeared—and never returned. I've said before, and I'll say it again: these methods are like learning to drive. If not handled with care, there's bound to be a crash. Always proceed cautiously. And if you do ask someone else to assist you, make sure they are trustworthy. Too many claim they can help when, in truth, they can't. Often, money—not healing—is their goal.

This, unfortunately, applies to many clairvoyants as well. There are some who are truly gifted and sincere—but also many who are not. I must admit, in my searching, I've wasted more money than I care to count. One particular disappointment stands out: a woman who came to our church claiming to have spiritual insight. We all paid for our sittings and waited for our turn. Before mine, a woman came out and shared some of what she'd been told. One line stood out—this clairvoyant had told her that, in her youth, she had been beautiful. It seemed heartfelt at first... until I heard her use the same line on nearly everyone. A clever opening, perhaps, but not exactly inspired! (Big grins.) It's best, if you're ever in a similar situation, to wear gloves or keep your hands hidden—people can read a lot from the state of your skin, jewelry, or how you carry yourself.

For my part, I never took up clairvoyance professionally. There were too many cracks in the system. Too many desperate souls searching for comfort, hanging on every word. And with a compassionate nature, it would've been too easy to tell someone what they wanted to hear—even if it wasn't true. That, to me, is dishonest. Giving the wrong answers, no matter how well-intended, is still misleading. And many who seek guidance are already fragile. They deserve better.

While I've enjoyed light-hearted sittings with friends, I always recommend writing your thoughts down as a form of self-reflection. No one ever needs to see it—just write whatever you feel. Let the paper absorb your pain, your hope, your questions. It's a powerful release. And if you need support, seek someone trained to help. They exist. One of my favorite sayings is, *"We are never alone."* I believe that deeply. We have our Helpers in spirit, and we also have earthly angels walking among us. People whose compassion overflows, who give and give without asking anything in return. I bet you know a few. I certainly do.

Does our subconscious guide us? Do we act out scripts written in past lives? Is the person we feel instant animosity toward—without reason—perhaps an enemy from another time? Who knows. We can only guess. But keep your mind open, your heart steady, and don't overthink it. One day, I believe, all will be revealed. And I'm quite willing to bet on that.

*****

Chapter 6:
From Sand to Soul

If I were you and you were me,
Our souls intertwined.
Two grains of sand united
Would make a greater mind!
And if that greater mind united
With another greater mind;
Eventually we would touch

Now humankind has become the beach, spreading across the earth—one body standing in love and beauty, recognizing every soul's worth.

It has become that shining diamond, with light so bright and strong. Its humble, lowly beginnings have helped spirit and soul along.

What a beautiful dream.

But then I ask—at what point did the darkness of nothing decide it would become something? What made it stir? What awakened it? Why?

I've asked myself this question over and over again. Still, in the dark, my searching soul remains. Maybe we aren't meant to know. And just as I begin to accept that, a little voice whispers, "Oh, come on, don't be slow—you really haven't got that far to go!"

Perhaps the answer is so simple that we overlook it. We make life harder than it needs to be. Each one of us is our own worst enemy.

Still, no matter what anyone says, it's not easy—there are so many trials and tribulations to face. But for me, reincarnation and karma have long been guiding lights. That's my path. It makes sense to me. Can we prove it? Maybe not, but we can try.

Take care, lovely people. Many say we are but grains of sand or facets of a diamond. What comforting images. Both hold deep meaning. Sand, when damp, holds firm. There's a lovely poem— "Footprints in the Sand." There are many versions, but the essence is always the same: that invisible energy—many call it God—carries us when we are too tired to carry ourselves. And while unseen, He leaves behind footprints to remind us we're not alone. It's a beautiful, uplifting reminder.

And the diamond—it speaks for itself. Each facet, when polished, reflects more light. United, they shine even brighter, like a spiritual beacon for others to follow. It radiates spiritual wealth. Just imagine: a radiant light soaring from the beach, stretching upward into the sky and beyond.

So, don't be afraid to visualize peace and understanding. This energy doesn't demand—it invites. It honors our free will, while quietly encouraging us to move forward... and not stay still.

I often talk about the darkness. When I was in junior school— around age 12, I think—I used to visualize nothingness. Not a thing. Just darkness. It was a strange feeling, to be honest. One day, our teacher asked us all to sit, close our eyes, and describe what we saw. Well, I saw darkness. Nothing. From that point on, the feeling stuck with me. I would sit quietly, visualizing that same nothingness. Just black. I'd put myself in the mind of, What if there was nothing? Absolutely nothing? It was a mystifying place to be, but maybe, just maybe, it was a good lesson in itself.

Looking back, I wonder if that teacher was into meditation. Whether or not the headmaster would've approved is anyone's guess—this was the post-war era, after all. Parents likely wouldn't have appreciated it either. Life back then was so two-dimensional. Just six or seven years after the war, people were still struggling. Towns and homes were being rebuilt. My own parents managed to get a prefab home, meant as a temporary shelter for the homeless.

Eventually, we moved to a house on a new estate—one named after the Royal Family.

It's possible that many eyes were opened through prayer during the war. When you're terrified, uncertain about survival, and grieving a loss, prayer becomes instinctive. I believe prayers made with genuine intent receive answers. I myself prayed often. Different life events led me there, and in the process, my eyes were opened to other aspects of existence.

Maybe that teacher had endured unspeakable trauma and was trying to pass along something he'd learned. I wouldn't be surprised if others found that same pathway during or after the war. Still, I don't think anyone in my age group really understood what he was doing. Meditation and visualization, in this part of the world, caught on slowly, gradually. But for me, that teacher gave me a glimpse. A tiny window. And over time, as I sat with eyes closed in that darkness, I began to notice light. Just a glimmer. It wasn't until I was married that it all started to make sense—an open book, if you will.

At that time, I was tied to orthodox religion. I gave it a lot of weight. But now? Now, I am a Free Thinker—free of any headings that lock the mind into one single narrative. I remember one day, one of my Helpers presented me with a thought: Why have headings at all? And if you think about it, aren't the headings what always get us into trouble? Who was the first to assign names and titles to things? Who spoke the first words?

Of course, we need headings and laws to survive—otherwise, chaos. We're not yet advanced enough to act in the interest of all without some form of guidance or discipline. Even with laws and the threat of punishment, people still stray. Still, I can see the logic behind not having headings. It would demand we act purely on reaction and conscience. Too complicated, if I'm honest. So here's what I say: Darkness—just become light. For all of us to win the fight. The fight for peace and understanding.

***

I sometimes wonder—what made superstition such a fixture in our lives? *Does it have any worth?* Don't walk under that ladder—so we don't. Don't step on that pavement crack—oops, too late! Avoid the number 13; it's unlucky. But what about those born on the 13th? Especially Friday the 13th—oh, that's a definite no-no! Spill the salt? Quick, throw some over your shoulder—what a waste! Whoops—hit the dog! There are so many dos and don'ts, it's a wonder we manage to get through life without tripping over every step.

I used to say I didn't believe in any of it… *mmm,* maybe I did more than I let on. Take this story, for example. One of my daughters was born with significant medical issues. At the time, I believed yellow was a healing color. I bought a yellow pram cover, convinced it would protect her. I used it constantly. I may even still have it, or perhaps I passed it on to my granddaughter when she had children.

We used to spend weekends in Teignmouth, Devon—a gorgeous stretch with an avenue of trees. The sun would shine through the leaves, creating a magical light. It was a place that made you feel alive. On one such day, I was pregnant with my son. As we prepared to leave, I noticed a yellow ribbon in my daughter's hair. I debated whether to take it along for good luck. I left it behind.

It was a beautiful day. Rob—my husband—never sped when the kids were in the car. In our courting days? We flew down those roads like mad things (smacked wrists), but once Sarah was born, that all changed. We drove cautiously.

That day, while cruising through that sun-drenched avenue, a car suddenly veered into the road and smashed into another. It flew across the lane. Had we been just one car ahead, it could've been *us*. My instinct? Get away, fast. But not Rob. He jumped out of the car and dashed across the road to the injured vehicle. It was mangled. He and another bystander pulled the driver and passenger out and moved them far from the wreckage—just in case it caught fire. Someone had already called for help, but Rob stayed with them until the ambulance arrived.

I didn't leave the girls. The road was far too busy. I just sat there—watching, waiting, breathing. And yes, I'll admit it again, I was glad to leave it all behind when it was over.

We were on our way to our static gypsy caravan. When we arrived and I took the luggage out of the car, there it was—lying on the ground. *The yellow ribbon.* It still brings tears to my eyes as I type this. That dear driver didn't make it. Rob had to go to court afterward, but I truly admired his bravery. We thought of the driver's wife often—she was okay, I believe. But still, I can't help but wonder: was it superstition, coincidence, or were we truly being looked after? It *could* have been us, to be honest. I have a feeling it was the driver of the car—the one who came out of the side road—who was at fault. And thankfully, he struck the car in front of us, not ours.

As we all know, it isn't always our own fault when these things happen. We just have to be grateful for safe travels, because anything can happen at any time. The sun still shone that day... as that soul was called *gently back to our Atom.*

***

Because we don't always *know,* it's not easy to figure out which path to take. So we carry on, hoping we're moving in the right direction. One day at a time—that's the only way, really. If we stopped to overthink everything, worried about every little thing, we'd never move forward. But remember this: there's *always* someone who will help. Don't be afraid to ask.

***

After a conversation with a friend, I had a strange little thought. We were talking about my ongoing battles trying to learn a new PC and its programs—*what a ride.* I joked about how things have changed. I told her about a time my granddaughter proved me wrong about something technical. After she explained and showed me the right way to do it, I had to apologize. She looked at me, smiled, and said, *"That's okay, Gran, as long as you learned something."* She was so young—*lol.*

In my defense, I started with just a pencil. In *my* day (and that was *long* ago—*big smiles*), pupils weren't trusted with anything else for a good while. Then came the pen and ink. I still remember the ink wells in our desks. One of the pupils had to fill them in every morning. We must've had a pen with a nib, though I can't quite recall the details. After the baby stages and graduation to big girls' school, we eventually got to use ballpoint pens. That was a leap!

My first mechanical encounter was with the typewriter. I attended Fulfords College to study shorthand, typing, and bookkeeping. My parents had been paying into a policy for years that covered education in two payouts—one at around age 15 or 16, and the other at 21. I ended up taking out three of those policies myself—for my own children.

The college was a grand old gentleman's residence, and we pupils sat in one of its large drawing rooms. It was run by a father and son. The father was decent. The son? *Say no more.* After two years of study, I entered the big, wide world (*lol*) and got my first job. I loved using the typewriter. We also worked with the dictaphone—typing up what had been recorded. That cut out the need for shorthand, which, I'll admit, suited me just fine. I much preferred completing tasks that way.

Years after getting married, I finally entered the world of computers. My first attempt? A word processor. I remember Sarah—my daughter—and I experimenting with it. We would end up in fits of laughter whenever we typed something, only to lose it all by pressing the wrong button. The fonts came from a changeable wheel—you had to buy them separately if you wanted anything beyond the default. I still have the italic font wheel somewhere. The machine itself? Long gone. Eventually, I sold it.

From there, I moved on to my very first computer. It was slow—very slow—and the screen was black and white until I eventually upgraded it to color. Over time, I graduated to faster machines, newer programs, and the ever-growing stack of CDs that came bundled with the systems in those days. I still have them all. Nowadays, of course, it's much easier; most apps are already built into the machine.

But circling back to my point—my colleague and I often wondered: *what's next?* So much has been invented for the enjoyment (and convenience) of mankind. And we have to admit, we've come a long way since just using a pencil! Who would've thought we'd live in a time where we can talk, face-to-face, with someone on the other side of the world? It's fantastic, to be honest—*such clever minds,* leading us toward what we can only hope is a greater glory. But then again... *what* will be the next step to take over? Will it be AI? Artificial Intelligence, as we speculated in our conversation?

Honestly, it doesn't bear thinking about too deeply. My theory—however quirky—is that we need to uplift this planet, to return it to its original position in the universe. And perhaps the universe still has further to travel. I can *see* this being a possibility, even though I know nothing factual. Like I've said before—I just love pondering these things for my own amusement. I seek, and I find my own explanations, knowing full well they are entirely mine and mine alone.

I have a home library full of books—many of which I still haven't read. Now, of course, we can access information online *just like that.* I do sometimes wonder what will happen to all my books when I pop my clogs. My family doesn't seem too interested in reading. It's all too easy these days with digital everything. Still, one of my favorite and most intriguing authors has always been Zecharia Sitchin. As far as I know, he wrote seven books. I have six, and I *have* read them—but it's been a long while. He's extremely descriptive, especially when it comes to the "whys and wherefores" of life—how it all began and so on. I must give them another go. Perhaps that's a good project for the winter months. The sun is out now, and we must make the most of that while we can.

One of his more striking theories—without going into the book itself, as I'd need to refresh my memory—is that all things were already underway *three thousand years* before the birth of Christ. I believe this theory is in *Genesis Revisited*, where he poses the question: *Is modern science catching up with ancient knowledge?*

One of his most fascinating books is *The Cosmic Code*, where he explores the idea that a group of extraterrestrials from another planet helped guide the evolution of life on Earth. He asks, *How did the master builders from the stars construct the miracle called man?* Could DNA—the very essence of life—be a kind of *cosmic code* linking Earth to Heaven, and man to "God"? Those are his editorial questions, taken from the back of his books.

Personally, I believe there's something of value in *all* of his writings. If I remember rightly, without double-checking, he suggests that these ETs merged with human life at the time. In doing so, the sacredness of their spiritual DNA mixed with the "lowliness" of the Earth's... and perhaps that was never supposed to happen.

Now, if we consider human evolution, did it begin in the sea? Were we born with gills? Did we evolve from apes, moving slowly up the ladder until suddenly there was a missing link? Theories go back and forth between evolution and creation. But if Sitchin is right, and some kind of union between species occurred, then perhaps *both* theories are correct. *Evolution and creation—working together.* Too far-fetched? Maybe. But it does offer some explanation. In my opinion, we make life unnecessarily difficult for ourselves. And inevitably, those difficulties become the source of division and argument between people.

It is said that the higher powers—the true overseers—were furious with the ones who interrupted the natural flow of evolution. If that's true, are those powers still working to repair the situation? Or worse—

are they still punishing us? We have to wonder: why *did* Earth separate from the rest of the universe in the first place? Was it a Big Bang? A cosmic collision? Did Earth break away from the original universe— or was it always meant to be apart?

Are we the ones at fault?

We could go on and on with our own thoughts—and I do love getting tangled up in them, even if they leave me in knots! But circling back to artificial intelligence for a moment—if we, in our fragile human state, can't uphold the intentions of the powers that be... will we eventually have to give in to the rise of AI? Goodness me! I already know, deep in my soul, that spirit can leave the body. So what's next? Transferring consciousness into an AI body? What would we even carry around with us in case that body collapsed? Only joking—just having a bit of fun! But really, could the intentions of the outer energies eventually become one? *Who knows.*

Sitchin, of course, based his work on a great deal of research. His books are worth exploring if one's even remotely interested in the whys and wherefores of life. He spoke often of the *Ancient Wisdoms*. And it makes me wonder: are we now circling back in time— experiencing things that already happened long, long ago? Is time reinventing itself? Are the inventions of today simply re-manifestations of what already exists in another part of the timeline?

I can't help but ask—*who* is guiding us? These brilliant minds on Earth—how are they seeing so clearly the next step in rebuilding? Is it subconscious? Are our Helpers silently leading us back to the Ancient Wisdoms? *Are* we living in a dimensional world? Are we catching up with versions of ourselves in another dimension? There's just so much to think about! Could a massive group of souls, sitting together on the sand under a canopy of diamonds, reach other dimensions? How many dimensions are even out there? So many questions—and now back to earth... the dishes are calling, lol. *Where's my knitting?*

I did start looking into the history of the pyramids at one point. Fascinating. Somewhere online—though I've since lost the link—there was a 3D video taken from inside one of them. It carried you down the ancient corridors of time. It would not surprise me in the least if they were tied to outside influences. So many of Earth's mysteries are right within reach, but still outside our understanding. Have you ever stood near an ancient structure and *felt* its energy?

When my daughter moved to a new town, there was a historic prison open to the public. I went in. I believe it was a round building in the middle of town. Inside, messages were scratched into the walls by past inmates—messages full of pain and despair. I touched one of the walls and felt a surge of sorrow, unmistakable and heavy. I walked over to the window and looked out, and the modern town seemed to disappear. I saw open fields, untouched by time. I imagined the building once stood alone before the town rose around it. *What* would we feel if we could touch the inner walls of the pyramids themselves?

In my book *Heaven to Earth*, I shared a story about Earth colliding with universal energy. A little Atom awakened, called to pull the energy free. It was written automatically—just my own thoughts. In it, that Atom—the one we named "God"—gently whispers, *Gently back, my beloveds. Gently back.*

While we live in a material world, we're always looking for things to guide us safely through the span of our lives. We seek upliftment to carry us forward. But I don't think I'd ever want to inhabit an AI body. And what about animals? Heaven forbid! I watched a program where someone tried to comfort a woman battling cancer. He believed animals had healing powers—that if a dog licked someone who was sick, it brought healing. People with closed minds laughed at him.

But if we're feeling low, lonely, or just unwell, the love of an animal can be absolutely transformative. They have a way of lifting our spirits. Dogs seem to *know* where to go. When they've been shown love, they return it a thousandfold. How many of us have pretended to cry, only to be instantly comforted by our pet? I believe that what

68

happens in those moments is that our spirits are lifted—and that opens the flow for healing energy to move. We shift from negative to positive. That, to me, is the magic.

As I've said many times, it's important to keep an open mind. This man on the program had clearly tapped into his inner emotions. He'd learned through experience. But many people are afraid of the unknown—they mock what they don't understand. That's why some people won't share their experiences at all—for fear of being laughed at.

There's also been debate about whether animals should be allowed into hospitals. I say *yes,* absolutely. I love all those heartwarming videos about animals helping others—whether humans or other animals. Even a soft toy can offer comfort. And yes, I have many! *Lol.* Anything that brings us closer to an understanding of life, anything that uplifts us, should never be dismissed just because it doesn't align with someone else's views.

We all have the right to choose our own way. But for me, an AI body would feel far too cold. An animal, by contrast, is warm, alive, and filled with soul.

And when all is said and done... will we still be around if that day ever comes?

***

Going back to the energies that linger in a room—what about the so-called ghost? I've mentioned before that I honestly believe *we ourselves* might be the ghosts in some of these encounters. Our astral body could be out and about, roaming freely, just having a bit of fun—*don't shout!* Many years ago, Rob and I stayed at an old inn in a historic town. The bedrooms weren't modern, but the beds were comfortable enough. That first night, though, I woke in the middle of the night and saw a ghostly figure pass through the room—a rather stout man. He looked as if he had come straight from Henry VIII's era.

69

Fascinating! I never did ask anyone about it, and truthfully, I can't even recall where it was anymore. But I wonder—*is he still there?*

So how was he formed? Was he drawn in from the astral planes? Was his appearance a reflection of the room's residual energy? Do we have two kinds of ghosts—one from the living and another from... somewhere else? Was that stout gentleman on his way to rebirth? Or just waiting for the right time to descend again? It's interesting, but truthfully, unfathomable to my mind.

***

Over the years, I've sat in many churches and attended numerous meetings with spiritual or religious intentions. One particular meeting stands out—for all the wrong reasons. It just didn't sit right with me. Still, I know that for others it brought great comfort, and that I could appreciate. The gathering took place outside of town. I went along with a couple of friends who attended regularly and spoke highly of it. But the adoration on display... it struck a wrong chord in me. The man leading the meeting seemed convinced he was some kind of savior—*arghh*. It felt like he had hypnotized the crowd.

Suddenly, people around me began lying down on the floor, chanting, shaking their limbs as if overtaken by something dark. A frenzy took hold of the room. I just sat there, my face no doubt a study in disbelief. Then the man came over to *me*! He said I looked troubled and claimed he wanted to save me. But he didn't *know* me. And if he could read minds, he would've walked away. I told him in so many words that I didn't need saving—and I was far more concerned for the followers sprawled across the floor.

Was I wrong? Perhaps. Who knows. But I *do* know this: I never went back. My solar plexus had picked up something I couldn't ignore. The energy was off, and I listened to that feeling. To me, it all teetered too close to a cult. I don't know how long it lasted after that, but I know I had no desire to find out. It's far too easy to get pulled into a negative situation when you're vulnerable. If we're lucky, we learn as we go.

***

I also recall attending another event—a completely different atmosphere. It was a meeting connected to Cliff Richard, who by then had become a Born-Again Christian. I loved his music; he's from my era, after all. I joined a coach filled with young Born-Again Christians headed to a stadium event. Though I wasn't officially part of the group, I was warmly welcomed. The journey itself was delightful—young people with guitars singing Christian songs the whole way. Their joy and connection were infectious.

When we arrived, the stadium was full. Cliff came out into the center of the field, sang, and praised the divine. The crowd was deeply respectful. Then he invited those who wished to be "saved" to come forward. The invitation was given gently—no pressure. Many people filed onto the field. My ego chuckled inside, thinking that if I had been the only one left in the audience, I *still* wouldn't have gone down. But for those who did, it brought visible comfort and joy. After the last person had walked out, the event closed. And what happened next was awe-inspiring—*total silence*. Thousands of people live in absolute stillness. It was overwhelming and beautiful.

***

Have you ever thought about how much our brains resemble a computer—especially when it comes to memory? Once we tuck a thought away, can we always retrieve it? As we get older, it sometimes feels harder to remember. Personally, I quiet my mind and wait for the pictures to reappear. Another trick I use—go through the alphabet, especially if I'm trying to recall a name. It often helps jog the memory.

At a seminar many years ago—led by a gentleman named José Silva—we were guided into a meditative state by one of the instructors. We'd been told beforehand that we would be doing a memory test, and I'll admit, I panicked a little. Memory had never really been my strong suit.

First, we had to make a list of ten random items. Then we made a second list and paired the items together, creating mental images of the two combined in unusual situations. For example, from the first list we had "elephant," and from the second, "cup of tea." So we visualized an elephant drinking a cup of tea. We did this for all ten pairs—while still in a deeply relaxed meditative state. After we were brought back to full awareness, we were asked to recall each item from the first list. The visualization helped tremendously—I managed to get nine out of ten correct. I only missed the tenth because I let my logical brain interfere instead of trusting my subconscious.

It was a powerful exercise—one I carried with me through the years. It made me realize how important it is to trust our *first* thought. That immediate impression likely comes straight from the subconscious.

Funny enough, I had once purchased a memory course—but I kept forgetting to do it! *Big grins.* The course was full of double lists and complex steps. We had to learn all the sequences before it became practical, which made it feel like more of a chore than a help. Honestly, it was wasted money.

The Silva seminar, on the other hand, was brilliant. It included a wide range of topics: meditation, healing, and simply being around like-minded individuals. I attended two or three in total. They were costly even then—goodness knows how expensive they are now! *Smiles.*

***

As I may have mentioned, I do believe our subconscious holds many answers. It stores all the *whys* and *wherefores*—things we've learned across time, or even echoes from another life.

It's often said that children are born with a deep inner wisdom. But as they grow, that wisdom gets buried beneath adult opinions and social conditioning. Of course, children do need some guidance, but the wise parent eventually learns to honor free will.

In today's world, we can learn so much from the young. And the young, in turn, can learn a great deal from the old. *Mutual wisdom*, I like to call it.

I wonder—if rebirth is a real phenomenon, could a soul carry its artistic skills or learned talents into the next life? We see young children today displaying incredible gifts—painting, music, and mathematics. And what about adults who suddenly discover a new skill or language they never consciously studied? Could these talents have been dormant, waiting to be unlocked?

Can hypnosis help us retrieve these fragments of past lives—memories or talents once held long ago?

Then again, maybe if we *knew* too much, faith would lose its meaning. The mystery of life might fade, and so would the rich conversations and deep friendships that arise from exploring these unknowns. Of course, with fewer debates, maybe we'd also have fewer enemies... *mmm*, there's a thought.

It's not always easy to have faith in humankind. We are, after all, imperfect beings. But raising our minds beyond the purely material requires exactly that—*faith*. And how we use it is entirely up to us.

"Seek, and ye shall find." We've all heard that before—but believe me, my friends, it's true.

Many moons ago, an acquaintance once remarked—thinking himself clever—that I was just "dead wood." *Mmm*. Oh dear... such ego. But—

> *If a friend should call you*
> *dead wood*
> *Would you complain, dead wood,*
> *What is within a name?*
> *Now let us consider the meaning of dead,*
> *When a person dies to a new world*
> *"He" is led.*

Now wood, wood is beautiful,
For as tree it once stood,
Mother Natures own blessings
Guarding all that is good.
Providing shelter for "Gods" precious birds,
Their singing so glorious beyond human words.
So my loves change bad to good,
Then reconsider Dead Wood, Dead Wood.

I wrote another little piece once—*If a friend should hurt thee with a useless word, just pretend you never heard!* When I look back on the words of my younger self, I'm so grateful we can progress. We *can* learn wisdom. We *can* start listening to that inner conscience that's always trying so hard to get through to us. In my opinion, there is a Source that's gently working to teach us all one thing—*universal love.* The powers that be surely have a purpose for each and every one of us.

Nothing is impossible. Sometimes things are said without thought—and sadly, I've no doubt that many of us have never made it past certain hurtful words. We've all been unreasonable at times. We've all said things we regret. That's why we must start by forgiving *ourselves.* Only then can we transform an insult into something greater.

Bad thought, in truth, becomes another's karma. And karma *does* work. Sometimes it's very subtle. Other times? *ARGHHH!* Take care.

***

We each have our own way of handling controversy.

***

I've just been trying to think about what I might write next. And wouldn't you know—it came to me while I was unloading the dishwasher! A little earlier, I'd been talking with a friend about John Masefield's poetry. We were trying to work out what exactly he meant in his piece *When I Am Dead*—the one I quoted at the beginning of this book.

At first, I wondered if he was a troubled soul, even though he was quite famous. But later, on reflection, when he said *"Let none see and then thank God that there's an end of me,"* I understood. He wasn't saying life ends. He was saying that *we* are spirit and soul, and we travel on. The *"me"* he spoke of referred to the *material self,* our temporary vehicle for this earthly journey.

In my view, he was in tune with the Infinite.

Why am I repeating this? Because in the moment I was focused on something entirely unrelated—*a practical chore*—I received an answer. My inner self handed me a fresh insight.

That's the wonder of it: when we *concentrate*, we open the gate. Ideas begin to trickle in. And often—if not always—there's another angle waiting for us to discover. Concentration cuts out the middleman. It invites direct communion.

***

I just found the following OBE entry, dated August 20th, 1993:

It was the strangest experience last night. Definitely not a dream.

I was in bed with Rob, but the bedroom was not our own. It felt vast, unfamiliar. I remember shouting in terror, afraid I'd disturb others. I was saying I loved him—meaning Rob—and I touched his face, trying to stay grounded. But a force kept erupting. At one stage, I even said I would not delve into the unknown anymore. I promised I'd leave it alone.

But it was definitely a force beyond myself.

One moment, I lay peaceful and still. The next, it was overtaking me. I was afraid—until I realized what was happening.

I was separating the bodies.

The moment I recognized it, I stopped resisting and let it carry me. I went out into the night, toward the stars. It was beautiful.

I remained fully myself—but then there was talk of another life. I was a man. And I felt a deep happiness at that realization. I was then in a room, fully conscious and curious. I tried to see what I looked like.

There, conveniently, was a mirror.

And there I stood. A well-built man with jet black hair. I looked Italian. There was a lot of chatter. I believe I was about to be punished for something. There was a gruesome-looking chair. The people around me felt both real and not real.

Very hard to explain, but I've had this phenomenon before. I was placed in a chair. I saw a contraption with steel teeth. I thought it was going to be put on my head—yet maybe it was placed on my hand? I remember feeling concerned, thinking I'd have to endure some pain, but nothing materialized. Then someone said *1945.*

I've had an experience before where I was told not to forget *1945.* If this were a past life, it's hard to understand because I was born in 1940. Still, it really *felt* like my experience. It was definitely not a sleep dream. What happened in 1945? *1945, please come alive.* Can the soul change bodies *after* birth? If so, who was the "me" born in 1940—and where did she go? *Lol,* the mind boggles. 1945— mentioned twice. The other time was really lovely. *Smiles.*

I've written before about the elderly gentleman who told me not to forget 1945. I must have a look and see if I dated that experience. Odd to have it twice. And this is the only experience where I remember *being male.*

Over the years, like many others, I've had several operations. My first was around the age of five—I had my tonsils out. I remember walking in a file with other children, all of us in long nightdresses. I was obviously placed on a table where something was put over my face. I was asked to count backwards. That was it. I woke up in a ward with the others. No other experience that I can recall.

I did, however, have an out-of-body experience during a tooth extraction—I've written about that: floating near the ceiling.

My first adult operation was in my forties. It was a common one, but it was still my first since the tonsils. My dear parents came to stay with me the day before. I was so nervous that I ate about six oranges in one sitting. The operation itself went fine. I woke up sore, but stable. I must admit, I was hoping to have an OBE—but if I did, I don't recall it.

The next operation was the beginning of a series of three follow-ups. This one was serious. I remember waking up calmly. The surgeon came in smiling. I looked at him and said, "I've seen you." He replied, "No, you haven't—I just saved your life."

I thanked him, of course. But that sense of knowing him lingered. As the surgery was an emergency, there's no way I could have seen him beforehand. Did I have an OBE and just not bring the memory back? Perhaps.

Substances can release the soul from the body. That's why certain mixtures can be dangerous. I believe many people have had spiritual experiences during medical procedures—they just may not understand the concept or realize it's a normal part of being human.

But we must be careful in this life. The wrong substances can bring in negative energies. Controlled medical environments are different. Just the other day, I read about someone who had been in a coma for a long time. When they finally woke up, they told their family they had heard every word. They were *aware* of everything.

And I believe this. I really do.

It probably depends on the dosage if controlled—or perhaps on the patient's own sensitivity if not. It's a lot to consider. Where do the souls of coma patients go while the body rests? I think that's why doctors often recommend talking to a patient—they *may* be able to hear us. I believe many do.

These thoughts only reinforce my belief that we are souls traveling inside heavy vehicles. I'd even go so far as to say we're capable of healing others in the sleep state—when most souls are likely freed. If we focus our intention on a loved one while asleep, maybe we can send healing energy. Hospitals today sometimes *induce* comas to allow the body to rest. I know this to be true.

And what do people say these days? *"Show me the receipts."* I have many!

Smiles.

Prayer helps. Let others act with you and for you. Souls united can help win the fight. We are never alone.

***

To be free, one must earn the rewards of life—whether as a *man,* a child, or a loving *wife.*

But when we label ourselves under rigid roles, we limit our duties to just that slice of life.

"Man and wife."

"Mother and child."

"Sister and brother."

Is there nothing more?

Surely there is.

If we lose each other, where do we look? *In a storybook?*

We live in a material world filled with labels. And yes, we *do* need some of them to survive and make sense of this part of our spiritual journey. But maybe—just maybe—we need to *let go* of some, just a little, to realize our own worth. Which way do we *want* to go?

If we are loved, then we naturally want to return that love—especially to those closest to us. So, do we go within?

My own experiences suggest that we *do*.

When we choose a label or heading, we often agree to follow the rules attached to it. That can be restricting. But if that label uplifts the spirit, and if we're willing to live by its values, then maybe it *is* the right path for us. Life's experiences often dictate the direction we must take.

I've mentioned my pendulum before—such a fascinating way forward. As I've said, it spoke to me. Was it my concentration opening a doorway to my inner knowing? The kind of inner knowing we're all possibly born with—but which we keep hidden from our everyday lives?

When we were young and pregnant, we used to determine the sex of our babies using a needle and thread held over the mother's head. I later replaced that with a crystal on a thread—my own pendulum. I had great success using it in a certain way. The focused concentration seemed to generate the energy required for answers. Words formed in my mind; they came fast, but I was able to write down their meaning after each session. I would write, then wonder—*does it make sense?* Here's something I wrote on June 20th, 1986:

Where does one start to tell the joys of the heart? Where does one travel from the very beginning to climb a mountainous hill—and yet, is it so simple? The trials and tribulations of living; have we really been fibbing to ourselves? Is it all a dream among life's many wonders? The universe... verse the old, old story of wondrous things in all their glory.

Now listen. Listen carefully. Let my pen be truth to thee. Let me tell you of an encounter with love—a holy thing. Though love can kill, as "Samid" says, for not all love is good. The greatest love we can possess is the kind that tells us not to fuss. But as human beings, it's hard. We rely too much on our lower selves and forget to look for the higher. Yet if we merge the two together, we may just reach perfection in all its glory.

The Deity, I'm told through loving thought, is a "mountainous" hilltop. But there's a mountain greater still. To reach that hilltop is already a blessing. We aren't always sure what our earthly lessons are, but to climb to the top is a goal of glory. Come, my precious loving creatures, let me tell you what Deity wants and knows. There is only one way to perfection. It's simple—but it takes a lot of detection. Holy love of a special kind. A forgiving love. One that blends both selves— the lower and the higher—an Astral Flyer. The lower self keeps us tied to this heaven-hell of Mother Earth. The higher self shows Hilltop spirits' beautiful worth.

To put it simply, was this message hinting that we must have a foot in both worlds? One in the material, one in the spiritual? Who knows, eh? What I do know is that it led me to Hilltop Manor—and pendulum love.

* * *

Alright, back to Earth—properly grounded now. I found another experience:

I was diving into an expanse of water. I kept going deeper and deeper. I became aware that I might not be able to turn back to the surface. Then I heard voices—they were discussing my body. They sounded concerned. I suppose I must've nearly drowned.

That same night, I was traveling in a coach or bus along what seemed to be a narrow mountain road. The vehicle suddenly hit something and took off. I knew—*this is it.* I couldn't believe it. We were flung into the air, and though I was high up, it wasn't the feeling of flying. It was the feeling of *dropping.*

I looked around and saw others falling too. I remember telling everyone not to panic, to stay calm, to relax their bodies so that when they hit the ground, they'd do so with ease. We all eventually landed.

I found myself in a building with three or four others—Sarah, my daughter, was one of them. I was congratulating them for surviving when I suddenly realized that Louise, my other daughter, was missing.

Panic set in.

I rushed to the window—ground level—to open it and run out. *(What happened to the door? Smiles.)* And there she was, walking toward me. Safe. I collapsed and sobbed. That part I remember vividly. I was also laid on the ground at some point, with water being pressed out of my body.

Later that same night, Louise and I were on a very long seesaw or swing. She was seated in front of me. I worked it higher and higher, so high we could see for miles around. I remember thinking that if I didn't pull my weight backward, we'd tip right over. We stopped. I asked if she wanted me to go again. I had just started when the vision disappeared.

I'm honestly not sure I slept at all that night.

Because I was also trying to find Rob, my husband, I had his hand and arm—trying to keep them wrapped in plastic or a towel. I was desperately trying to hold his flesh and muscle together so it could be stitched back on. At the same time, I was trying to care for my grandson. I had to leave him with a bottle while I searched for Rob— *before it was too late.*

Oh boy—what a night.

Was this all symbolic? A family accident? Were we all somehow linked in a shared reincarnation? Had we been together before?

***

Three great things to possess in life: love, loyalty, and wisdom. Wisdom is the most important because you need it to know how best to handle the other two.

So—gently back (*smiles*) to the pendulum.

There was a time when it took me into what seemed like nothingness. Was that the result of me trying to discover what such a place might be like? Well, I'll tell you this—it was *very* lonely. Total darkness. And yet, oddly enough, my subconscious *knew* where I was. I knew how to get myself back to reality.

On another trip, I became conscious of a beautiful, strong light. I didn't enter Pandora's Box, though—it didn't feel like the right time. The perfection I sensed was overwhelming... almost frightening. I had a thought: *If we had perfection, wouldn't we eventually grow bored?* Maybe it's the *trials* that let us know we're alive. Maybe it's the struggle that helps us recognize our worth.

Our physical bodies—our vehicles—stay with us while we sign into this classroom of Earth. Maybe we're here to *earn* that perfection. And maybe, just maybe, we'll know when the time is right to bring heaven to earth—to *become* what we truly are.

In that second experience, I felt I was being led. I wasn't afraid.

There's an interesting video online right now—it talks about simply *being*. Just being in tune with the infinite. Beautiful idea. But for me, it veers away from the hope that we'll be reunited with our loved ones who've already left us. Perhaps that's where the idea of *steps* comes in. One step at a time. Each step reveals that we're never really alone, and that we *do* have a duty—to ourselves, and to the soul's path.

So climb that golden ladder. Find your little Atom. Then carry on—out into the universe.

***

Hey folks, are you still with me? (*Big smiles.*)

I do chew over a lot of what I read or watch. I *love* the challenge— as I've said many times before. I do have deep faith in the subconscious.

***

Have we ever wondered about multiple personalities?

You might remember my earlier experience—being in *three places at once*. I was in control, I knew it was happening, and I hoped I could revisit that moment someday. But I never did. After a while, the pendulum stopped working in the same way. Perhaps the energies shifted. Or maybe my subconscious decided it was time to come *back down to earth*. Life needed my attention.

I find multiple personalities absolutely fascinating—especially if the person isn't suffering from it and remains aware. I haven't researched it fully... yet. Maybe one day.

***

Something I *am* grateful for—as someone who questions the "whys" and "how comes"—is the work of archaeologists. Their efforts bring the past back to life. What a reward, to uncover ancient treasures, long forgotten. Skeletons of all sizes? Proof, perhaps, of stories that once seemed implausible.

We're used to seeing life as it is now—predictable, structured. Anything different can make people uncomfortable.

I've mentioned Zecharia Sitchin's work. I haven't read all his books—maybe now's the time to start again. He talks about giants walking the Earth. And yes, I believe skeletons have been found.

In one of my OBEs, I remember standing inside a very tall building. There was no roof. But peering *over* the top was a face. A *giant's* face, perhaps—judging by the height of the walls. I felt I was being observed. And yet, I wasn't afraid. I seemed to be completely alone, but safe—inside those walls.

Could this experience support my idea that the spirit incarnates into different *vehicles*? Some bodies—some "vehicles"—may be too heavy for this planet's conditions. So the soul simply exits, and those species vanish altogether. Makes sense, doesn't it?

Sitchin's work is worth studying—but it has to be done with an open mind. He did real research. And honestly, I can accept much of what he presents.

He talks about souls being transported to other planets. His theories are "fact-filled," backed by ancient artifacts and modern maps. They inspire a kind of journey—*from the dawn of time to the new millennium.* His books are still like new on my shelf. Maybe I should air them out a bit—give them some light and life again.

***

Years ago, I bought a book called *The Corner Stone.* I was so impressed with it—but I lent it out and never got it back. It dealt with the fall of the Angels. I've searched for another copy, but it doesn't seem to be in circulation anymore. I'd love to compare its message with other writings.

When I told someone about its contents, they responded negatively. They didn't even listen. Their minds were already closed.

That's always been a bit of a tragedy in life, hasn't it?

We really mustn't let others disillusion us. Maybe their pathway just leads down a different fork in the road.

I firmly believe we're being guided—guided by teachers of great understanding.

As Zecharia Sitchin points out, *"oracular dreams and three-dimensional visions were some of the ways by which mankind was given access to extraterrestrial secret knowledge."* We, the little grains of sand—facets of a greater diamond—aren't yet wise enough to argue over things we don't fully understand.

Sitchin's books are easy to read and cover a vast spectrum of thought and research. I do wonder, will I have time to read them all? (*Smiles.*)

The quote I just shared comes from his book *Divine Encounters: A Guide to Visions, Angels, and Other Emissaries.*

We're fortunate, aren't we? To have people like him—people willing to dedicate their lives to research, to ask the questions many fear, and to generously share their findings with the rest of us. Still, I often wonder: who were they in past lives? That's assuming reincarnation is real, of course.

But to me, the presence and recognition of such great minds only *strengthen* the likelihood that it *is.*

We have John Masefield—sharing his depth through poetry, echoing the voice of the infinite. And we have Sitchin—offering visions of cosmic truths unearthed from ancient wisdom. For now, these are two of my favorites. I've also noticed Sitchin says: *To have eternal life, one must have a foot in each dimension.*

***

I can accept that. I can accept Sitchin's theory, and so—once again—I find myself returning to the question of *why*. Why do we weep so bitterly over the inhumanities of Earth, when the answer might be so simple?

We are spiritual beings, but we get lost in the wheel of life.

If only we could open the door... we might see that we've lived many lives before. That we've already *learned* many things.

We may appear distant, fragile, and overwhelmed while walking this Earth—but there *is* a source that knows, that understands every soul's worth.

So how do we help another to stop grieving? To stop drowning in sorrow?

The mind, after all, is an illusion. It deceives, distracts, and distorts. But the *true* spiritual being—the soul that lies within—knows only good. And yet, it understands *sin*.

That's what compassion is.

We tend to interpret everything through the material mind. We default to our human conditioning. So when we see a smile, a gentle love, or a kiss shared between two souls—we're too quick to judge it as improper, misread, or amiss.

We forget to recognize the *universal* love that surrounds us. That holds us up. That sees no labels and no limits—only life and light.

There are many kinds of love in one lifetime:

—The love for a partner, whether husband or wife.

—The love for our children, whose lives we nurture and shape.

—The love for the self, which takes the longest to understand.

This little piece you've just read came to me after experiencing a moment of jealousy. It caused unrest in the heart. And as it often does, it puts the human mind completely to the test.

|On **29ᵗʰ May 1993,** I wrote the following:

A good writer must be able to stand emotionless outside of all things; to stand and survey, then gradually let one atom of their being travel into the emotions of "man."

To reveal how I feel, I must steal the sufferance of man. To touch that emotion as deeply as the ocean, I must stay as still as I can.

It takes one braver than I—because if I move, I will cry. For man's suffering is real. And I know how they feel, for I am part... with an emotional heart.

So for a while, I will stay free. And then let me see—can I help, can I save... am I so brave?

Stay free. Stay free. Let me see, let me see. Stay calm. Stay calm. An emotional act will destroy, not save. Don't rave, don't rave. I am trying to learn. Don't yearn, don't yearn.

Breathe in deep. Don't sleep. Don't weep. Just breathe deep. Exhale—you won't fail. You won't fail. Don't wail. Don't wail.

Try again. Over and over. Come on, my gentle people, follow me. Follow me and you will see…

That emotions aren't real— They just make us feel The misery of man.

The truth is deeper. So much deeper. You are the reaper— A beautiful reaper of luxurious blessings. You and I—so please, do not cry.

You have lost a child… a loved one… your home…

But your being is the truth.
The part that will survive.
You are alive—along with the rest.
You and I… we are being put to the test.

We must do our best to realize… life is a disguise.
We only see with mortal eyes.

Go within. Go within. It is no sin to want to win
The blessings of life.

I do not want to speak of soul.
I do not want to speak of spirit.
I do not want to speak of religion.
There is only us if we cannot see.

My suffering people—
I see. I see.
We are free. We are free.
Alas, my loves, I suffer with thee.

Wait, my love—what is this I feel?
I have moved. For my tears are real.

Stay calm. Stay calm.
Remember the Almighty will.

***

I don't know anymore how to name these revelations. Because the moment I speak of them, I'm forced to accept a heading.

I have to say, *"I believe."*
I have to talk about *"God,"*
...the devil,
...the savior of man.

I have to choose a side for an intelligent debate—
But the idea of winning? It brings me neither love nor hate.

I am still.
I am calm.
I am me.
I am *free.*

Free.
That is me.

(*Smiles.*) All that... just to say *I am free.*

I think, at that time, I was simply experimenting with my own thoughts.

And yes—I still agree: to write honestly, one must learn how to stand outside their own feelings. If a writer lets the tears flow, they'll soon run out of paper. But then again, it depends, doesn't it? On the individual... and the subject.

***

In 1993, I wrote about a film I had just watched. It must've struck a chord with me. It sounded fascinating—clearly written by someone with a deep inner knowing about reincarnation. I do believe many writers, whether consciously or not, bring their past lives to the page.

The story followed a selfish man who dies, only to be reborn as a woman. His soul must redeem itself. As a woman, he experiences childbirth… and then death.

What an extraordinary concept.

I wish I could remember the name of the film—or who was in it! (*Smiles.*)

***

YouTube covers a lot of subjects—many of which I'm quite interested in. One in particular comes under the heading: *Do those who have passed get in touch with their loved ones in the dream state?* Now I would definitely say yes.

I've had many dreams—both ordinary and vividly visual—where I was with loved ones who've passed. Most of these dreams seem to come around Christmas time. As I've said before, Christmas was always very important to us. Since marrying Rob, we made sure to celebrate it as a family, extended and otherwise. Some years it was at our home, other times at my parents'. From that point of view, I believe my dreams are telling me that we're still within reach of each other.

My first job, in my teens, was in a typing pool at a major insurance company. The building had several departments, and many friendships were formed across the different sections. The first friend we lost in that group passed away from cancer.

There were a couple of years when several of us married our partners. I remember this particular lass very well. Her favorite perfume was *Tweed.* She was popular and well-loved. After she got married, she left the company. While she was single, she lived with her parents in a care cottage at the end of Exminster Hospital. Her brother was a footballer.

Years later, as I began researching my family history, I found out that Rob's grandparents both worked at that very hospital. That's where they met and eventually married. Small world!

After our colleague passed, the years went by, and I lost touch with most of the people from the typing pool and other departments. Much later, while working in North Devon, my job involved visiting customers at home. And after many years had passed—since both my time at the insurance company and my current job—I had a very vivid dream.

It was about that same lass from the typing pool who had died. I couldn't understand why she appeared in my dream. We hadn't been in contact in years. We had met briefly before her death at a reunion dinner (we used to have those with folks who'd stayed in touch). But that was all.

A while later, I started working with some new customers—who happened to live just a few doors down from Rob and me. As I took their information, it came to light that the woman of the house was the *aunt* of the soul who had visited me in my dream. Quite fascinating, to be honest.

Even though I had worked with her niece, we had lost contact after our marriages. The aunt didn't stay long in the house—it was just a short-term arrangement—so we lost touch again. Still, the timing of that dream and the connection was quite something.

There's more.

We continued having reunions—usually once a year. Most of us were from the typing pool, but a few people from other departments would join as well. One night, I had a visual dream. In the dream, I was walking out of a room when I heard a voice. I turned around, and there—sitting on a chair—was a man who used to work in one of the other departments at the insurance company.

To be honest, I don't recall ever talking to him when we worked together. But there he was in my dream, just as I remembered him from years ago—unchanged. I didn't say anything to him, but *he* spoke to *me*. He said he was worried about the children.

It's possible he felt safe talking to me because his wife was someone I still saw at reunions. At the time, I chose not to say anything to her. I wasn't sure how people felt about those kinds of experiences.

Two years went by.

At another reunion, I happened to sit next to his wife. It was really the first time we'd had a proper conversation. We chatted, and eventually, I plucked up the courage to tell her that I had seen her husband. This was two years after the dream, remember.

To my surprise, she told me that the children had been having a bath, and they said they *saw* their grandfather. I can't quite remember all the details now, but there seemed to be genuine concern at the time.

***

As we've all aged, the reunions have slowly faded. They carried on for years, but a few of our group have now been gently called back to their heavenly home.

If only we could all gather one more time—just to sit together and talk about positive thoughts. To ask: *Do we believe, or do we not?*

As I've said before, I believe. In the instances I've shared, clues were given to me—clues through departed souls. Souls, I wasn't even particularly close to when we worked together. Yet they reached out somehow.

***

Back in 1998, I wrote:

Lately, I've been trying hard to go back in time, for I feel that time isn't real—it's man-made. "Man," many moons ago, looked up at the stars, the sun, the moon, the universe. And then set a scale to live by.

The trouble is, a day isn't long anymore. A week feels like a day, a month like a week, and a year like a month. It's as though time is collapsing in on itself—and eventually, all will be as one.

But what's the point of that, I wonder?

A year will be a day. "Man" will be born in the morning and die at night.

Is the universe in such a hurry?

So where are you taking us? We can only move with time as it stands. We cannot make demands—for they are never met. At least... not as yet.

***

HIDDEN TREASURES

When I read over words from the past,
I realise that my thoughts were meant to last:
To lose a friend is not the end.
We are born in this world as tiny child; and yet,
Within our being the truth and wisdom; we cannot forget.
As tiny child in innocence; we start to learn again.
But little do we know it is just a material brain.
Spiritual knowledge is tucked away,
For on the earth we have to find the way
To unlock that spiritual door.
Let me see my friend; at the age of one
What have we learnt;
A step on the ladder to our heavenly home.
A step or two to see us through; and then
Our tongue connected to the mind
Baby words of love we find.
Our earthly parents have learnt before;

The things we try; the points we score.
The years roll on from child we are led,
Till on our own spiritual food we are fed.
For some just a taste for others; plenty.
It may take a year; it may take twenty.
But plod on dear friends; plod on.
This worldly place we call Mother Earth;
Is full of "God's" love;
It will meet each ones worth;
It is only a second in our spiritual life;
We are but lent to each other;
Even man and wife.
A tiny child we may love; but not own.
For its pathway it must tread spiritually alone.
A friend we may cherish but not possess.
For time changes the mind; I must confess.
When all is considered if we strive for perfection
We are on our own with "Gods" love for protection.
But whilst here we cherish each other;
Be it friend, child, sister or brother.
The hardest thing to realise is; that we must let go.
For our goal in life is to be part of the "Whole"
In equality.

For years, I've seemed to follow the suggestion of reincarnation and karma. Interestingly enough, my mind doesn't seem to have changed—I'm still listening to my *subconscience*, hoping it's on the right track (smiles). Who knows, eh? As I've said over and over again, we each walk our own path.

I once had an OBE where I was literally seated in a UFO with my family. We seemed to be traveling somewhere—for some reason, we were being saved. I never did find out from what.

***

Many speak about twin souls—soulmates. Now the challenge: is it to find one's soulmate while on planet Earth? I was once told that two loving people, who had passed within months of each other, had been joined together after death. If that's true, it's understandable— they were like Derby and Joan while here on Earth.

That thought just opened up another avenue of reflection for me. In order for spirit to move forward—beyond the first level of understanding—do souls need to be joined, secured with one or more others, enabling the pure *mass* to travel on to the next level?

So much to think about, really. When the time comes, I'm sure many will smile and realize that we had the answers all along.

On the other hand… what *are* the answers? (big smiles)

> *I had a dream; an astral dream,*
> *Where things are not what they would seem.*
> *To me they are real; to others they are not.*
> *I dreamt and knew what I heard was true.*
> *So now I will ponder and see it right through.*

May all your dreams be great; with love.

THOUGHTS

I would love to think that I could prove karma and reincarnation— but I can't. I can only reflect, for my own benefit and spiritual values.

I know many people struggle to understand why some suffer while others seem to have a straightforward life. That alone suggests there's a reason. But what is the reason? Some say yes—there is reincarnation. Others believe there's no need to be reborn—that we only get one life. But what about those whose lives are deeply negative? Where they are the ball, and others are the skittles—knocking them out one by one, with no thought of retribution.

So many people do just that. What happens then? Is that soul destined for obliteration—no second chances, just… gone? What was the point of its birth? Are souls the very source of the universe? Are some single souls born pure, while others need multiple lives to obtain that purity?

Once again, every perspective has its own reasoning—if we keep our minds open.

When we reach universal knowledge, do we continue past Heaven, so to speak? One step at a time, sweet thought… one step at a time.

In my book Heaven to Earth, I introduce, along with my family— for we are as one—our little Atom. He was awakened from a deep sleep. He was the only one conscious. He chose to leave the peace of simply drifting through the universe. A great collision had occurred; energies had been separated. A voice kept urging him to act, to repair the damage, to pull the energy through—to allow the Whole to move on. We named him "God."

***

I watched two films recently that brought tears to my eyes. I didn't want either of them to end (big smile). Have you ever seen a film that stays with you? That lingers long after the credits roll?

The first was about a soul plagued by horrific visions of another family from the past. She experienced their trauma as if it were her own. Eventually, she went searching—wondering if they were still alive. And, of course, she found them—aged and scattered. The beauty of the film was in watching her bring them back together after decades of separation. Her analyst described the visions as either reincarnation or spirit communication. Right up my alley—I believe in both.

The second was about a young man who, after being in a coma for five years, woke with psychic abilities. He gently helped people in need, preventing tragedies before they happened. The main event, though, cost him his own life—but in doing so, he saved a corrupt man who had plans to become president. His visions were disturbing and powerful. You were left wondering: How?

***

On April 19, 1907, according to Wikipedia, Joan Grant—pen name Joan Marshall Grant Kelsey—was born in London to John Frederick Marshall and Blanche Emily Hughes. Her father was a wealthy man with dual U.S.–British nationality. In 1927, she married Leslie Grant, later Charles Beatty, and finally Denys Kelsey in 1960.

Joan described her mother as having second-sight visions, and from girlhood, she too experienced what we might now call parapsychological phenomena. Friends described her sensitivity as eerie. Understandably so—at the time, such gifts were feared. Thankfully, the witch hunts are over, though misunderstanding life itself still causes many to suffer.

Some people are just born with gifts. And when those gifts are used for good, they truly are blessings. I don't discredit religion, but I do believe it has much to answer for. It has been used—and abused. In many cases, the true essence of spiritual practice has been lost— replaced by fear and ego. On the other hand, sometimes we have to "let go and let God," to find peace and carry on through our trials.

Joan, with her sensitivity, became a great novelist. Her path even crossed with the legendary H.G. Wells through her father's friendship with him. And don't we wonder where his brilliance came from? His superior knowledge, his imagination, his ability to lead us into mysterious and thought-provoking places? Apparently, Joan was cautious about discussing her spiritual gifts. Even H.G. Wells warned her when she was only sixteen: if she didn't have the strength to endure others' laughter, she should keep her thoughts private. It took her twenty years to speak openly about what mattered to her.

I believe many of us feel that same caution. We fear judgment. And too often, people forget that everyone is entitled to their own beliefs. I'm sure we've all been guilty of laughing behind closed hands, of dismissing what we don't understand.

Joan became a *truth teller*—openly sharing her spiritual experiences and writing about them in depth. Her story included the fact that she and Leslie, her first husband, spent twenty-five days in Egypt. She later expressed regret that, during that one and only visit, she had no idea she had once lived there in a previous incarnation.

Joan's first novel, *Winged Pharaoh* (1937), was written in what she described as a hypnotic state. I believe she was suggesting that the novel was a reflection of her *own* past life—an experience from long ago, brought forth through deep inner memory. She seemed to speak with conviction and clarity. This was a woman who truly *believed* in reincarnation.

What a rare and beautiful gift it must have been to know H.G. Wells—and other great minds with profound stories of their own. One wonders—where did *their* gifts come from? Was it their subconscious? Was it that inner knowing—the truth that yes, their experiences *were* real?

We each have our own lifeline to the *Whole*. And I must admit, I feel a quiet thrill being able to identify with some of these timeless souls and their journeys.

But in today's world, it's harder to relate. Fear seems to rule the collective mind—especially fear of the unknown. People are afraid to speak of the soul, to name what they cannot prove. But we are *never* alone.

When my grandfather passed away back in 1967, I wrote the following. And in doing so, I came to a very personal realization: we each must accept our losses—and carry on—while our loved ones rest safely in the arms of Angels:

A soul is lost, I count the cost;
No more tomorrow, just grief and sorrow;
No more laughing, teasing, chaffing;
No love to borrow, just grief and sorrow
But wait my love, your soul above.

In peace it stays for endless days;
The grief is mine yes mine; not thine,
In selfish ways for endless days;
I weep for me, yes me not thee;
But the loss is true for I lost you.

Sentimental, I know—but it *is* hard to lose a loved one. Through my reflections and rhyme, I came to understand something gentle but powerful: the soul carries on, even as we grieve the loss.

I truly believe the soul rests in peace before beginning its journey back to Earth—*if* it so wishes. And I often wonder if it's just as hard for the departed to leave us as it is for us to let them go. Sometimes, we see tears in their eyes. Other times, a quiet smile as they reunite with those who passed before them.

There's so much to consider, so many unknowns. But somehow, the depth of the mind—the quiet wisdom of the soul—is really kind.

It *knows*.

Listen Within

To listen within to the still, still voice
To listen within, find "God's" love and rejoice;
Seek the Christ Spirit in thy higher self;
In God's love, you will find a pure, pure wealth.

....

DARK

Be not afraid of black, my friend
Be not afraid of the night.
The darkness that for some is the end;
Should surely turn to light.

*****

MEDITATION

I once saw a man dressed in white—not the Nazarene—leading a donkey. His head was covered with something like a turban, though not quite. I greeted him: "Greetings, my friend. Do you wish to speak?"

He nodded and replied, "The road is long and hard to travel." I looked ahead and saw the path stretch endlessly into the horizon. Still, he plodded on, calm and sure.

"You see, my friend," he said, "if a gem is worth having, I will go to the ends of the earth to find it. I will ask the way—and then, clear as day, my feet will follow the light. I kneel before thee—"

(A beautiful fragrance filled the air.)

"—and I kiss the ground, for I know God's beauty lies here to be found. I am thee. I am me. I am fame and fortune. I seek truth. Follow me, little one. Tread carefully—I will not lead thee astray. I will show you the way. Come, follow. Cosmic thoughts will be thine.

You have walked this path once before. You now return to walk it once more. So… find peace."

***

I used to meditate often. When one learns the art of letting go—of stilling the mind—there's so much to discover. Eventually, you begin to rest in that magical realm of silence. The energy becomes alive around you. To me, that energy *is* God—not "man," but Life itself.

As we soften, quiet, and simply *watch*, we notice what comes to mind. Visions arrive on their own, unforced. If I had asked a question beforehand, sometimes I'd receive an answer—if not, then perhaps it wasn't yet time. Meditation teaches patience. I've taken many journeys this way—purely through raw, unfiltered meditation. (Smiles.) It's an art, no doubt, but one well worth practicing.

You can even tune in—through the solar plexus—to another's feelings. It's like spiritual empathy.

So perhaps this was how the great masters did it. Did they meditate for their answers? Were their teachings just their own subconscious rising to the surface?

I've often said: we *do* know what life is all about—we've simply forgotten. And we must earn the key that unlocks the doors of earthly wisdom. Every person has their own skills. Every small thought matters.

***

Let's pause and breathe a little. In my book *Heaven to Earth*, I tell the story of my son's operation. He was only five when he underwent surgery for a hole in his heart.

Before the operation, he had a vivid dream. In it, he was caught in a battle—fighting surrounded him—and he was shot in the heart. He insisted that was why he was born with the hole.

I never pushed my beliefs on my children. But I remember him slipping into what felt like a trance while at the hospital. I had to call a nurse to gently bring him out of it.

Was it the medication? Possibly. But perhaps… it was something more. He was only five. Children, they say, are closer to the veil. They often carry gifts the world forgets to honor.

Still, life went on. We laughed a lot, as families should—even at silly things. What others might call childish or ridiculous, we found hilarious.

While looking through a little notebook filled with sentimental and funny moments, I found one entry that made me chuckle. If I remember right, this was during the era when streaking was all the rage…

Our Son, the Streaker

Our son has decided to keep in the trend,
Discretely, he did it for fear of his end.
I bathed him and dried him,
Then sent him downstairs;
For poppa to dress him before saying prayers'
Alas, the dear chap did open the door,
He ran down the street,
To my mighty roar:
Dad, quick, catch him
Run as fast as you can".
I felt a bit mean for spoiling his plan,
But the sight of his bare bot rushing around,
Would have made the Wades the talk of the town!

I have to add—he was very young at the time! It was around 1975. (Smiles.)

Still in 1975, I found a sweet little note I had written on behalf of my son. We had just spent Christmas together, as was tradition in our family:

***

Dear Grannies and Grandads,

I'm writing to say thank you all for Christmas Day. The whole holiday, I truly enjoyed. I know for sure I was a good boy—my daddy says so!

Mummy loves me... at least I think she does. Yes, I'm sure—because I help her every day, you see. She often says, "What would I do without you?" (She says something about peace, but I'm not sure what she means.)

I tried scrambling an egg the other morning. Mum was upstairs cleaning the awning. She spoiled my fun, I must admit—dashed down the stairs, then had a fit!

(Spoilsport… after all, Dad cleaned the saucepan and the cats ate the egg.)

Daddy often chips in. I hear him say, "What the devil is that boy playing?"

(I think he thinks I'm going to be a musician.)

My sisters love me—I know they do. After all, when they chased the rabbit, I went too.

(Though I never told them it was me who let it escape in the first place… whoops!)

Anyway, I think I must close. It's time for bed. I'm feeling weary and must rest my head.

Goodnight. God bless.

Lots of love,

Your loving grandson

***

So many tales to tell…
Of life in all its glory—
Happy, sad,
And always the old, old story.

***

I often wonder—what disaster of their time prompted those learned people to write their stories?

Were they responding to the troubles of their world? It's clear they had a deep desire to share something meaningful… To leave behind a message that still speaks.

20th Olympics 1972 Munich

I weep for humanity, it's kind so untrue;
I weep as I watch the ceremony through;
United, they marched or thought they were so;

But sadness and tears they were soon to know.
Alas, alas, I wonder why?
It started all so very well;
How would it end who could tell?
Love and friendship should always be;
Results for all clearly to see.
Alas, alas, they had to die;
Let us all stop and think;
What to do before we sink;
How to pass the word around;
Rise above the falling ground;
Alas alas not all will try;
Just one tiny little word;
Said so loud it will be heard;
One so pure and white as fleece;
Say it now and then find PEACE;
And then I will no longer cry.
So many souls lost, so many tears shed—
But back to our Atom, they were gently led.
I wonder how many stayed—
In the tranquility of knowing that spirit keeps on growing.
How many descended the ladder again?
To Earth—to remain—
A different body, a different path.

As I've said before, I tend to write first and research later. It's surprising how much a person can discover simply by trusting their intuition—the intuition I believe stems from the *subconscience*, our *inner being*, which many people don't even realize is part and parcel of who we truly are. We just have to learn to use it to our advantage.

I've recently started reading a book about the remarkable talents of Edgar Cayce. He was, once again, one of those gifted souls who tapped into the same source that many other learned people have drawn upon. And I have to say—I understand those talents. I find him incredibly interesting. He often spoke about the *inner self* and pointed out how so many people are unaware of the treasure they already hold within.

Many know that Cayce would put himself into a hypnotic state before his readings. He always maintained that he never remembered what was said once he returned to his normal state. His readings touched on everything from distant healing to tuning into another person's emotional or spiritual makeup. By all accounts, he achieved great results.

According to Doris Agee, Cayce was born on March 18, 1877, and passed on January 3, 1945, in Virginia Beach, Virginia. Ah! Ah! *Another 1945!* (Smiles.) Before each session, he reportedly met with an elderly gentleman in his subconscious vision—a ritual of sorts, a protocol that seemed to set the tone for his success.

In Doris Agee's book, Cayce constantly references the *unconscious mind*. And just like many other spiritually aware individuals, he saw it as central to understanding life's deeper meanings. When so many of these wise souls speak of the same thing, you begin to wonder—were they all trying to show us something?

Maybe they were. Maybe they were trying to help us remember that yes, we *do* have an unconscious mind. And yes, it *can* guide us. It knows, and it understands part of the grand plan for our spiritual progression—here and beyond.

But because we're mere mortals, none of us can say for sure that we know the way. Even so, if we choose to step onto the spiritual plane of understanding, we stand a far better chance of progressing. That first step is within us all—a step onto the golden ladder. First, back to *our Atom*. And then—who knows? Look for the ladder that glows.

Many have gone before us, and many are still trying to guide us. They've left their footprints in the sand. We can try to walk in them—before the waves wash them away.

****

www.ingramcontent.com/pod-product-compliance
Lightning Source LLC
Chambersburg PA
CBHW020321130626
46549CB00003B/956